17078

# WEAVING CREATIVITY into EVERY STRAND of Your CURRICULUM

## Dr. Cyndi Burnett and Julia Figliotti

A  Publication

# ACKNOWLEDGMENTS

To our colleagues, Andy Burnett, Eileen Burnett, John Cabra, and Susan Keller-Mathers: Thank you for lending your eyes and opinions to our book.

We would also like to extend a special thank you to everyone who contributed to this book: creativity experts, educators, parents, students, professionals, and more.

Mario O. Aguirre González, Garth Aldrich, Karina Loera Barcenas, Najja Bouldin, Mike Bridge, Clay Bunyard, Matthew Christian, Heather Clemmer, Shantel Coleman, Christina Coyle, Marta Davidovich, Daniel Laó Dávila, Urbie Delgado, Barbara Denney, Cecelia Fichter DeSando, Kathysue Dorey, Newell Eaton, Claire Lewis Evans, David Eyman, Amy Kashuba-Shanahan, Aubrey Kenneth Fisher, Janice Francisco, Robert Frantz, Jonathan Garra, Mark Gerl, Karen Gibson, Dan Greenberger, Jane Harvey-Gibbs, Amy Griesmer, Katie Haydon, David Hoffman, Mim Hoffman, Dixie Hudson, Stanton H. Hudson, Jr., Sasha Johnson, Miriam Kelley, Felix-Kingsley, Dee Langsenkamp, Josh Mahaney, Ismet Mamnoon, Mario Manzi, Maria Marinaccio,

Brad Matson, Daneen McDermott, Daniel Medeiros, Mattia Miani, Mark Morvant, Kimberley Murch, Dana Myers, Jean Nitchals, Paul Nordquist, Kelly O'Toole, Tony Pagliaroli, Caroline Pakel, Celia Pillai, Jenn Portratz, Lina Pugsley, Donna Ray, Julia Roberts, Mariana Rodrigues de Almeida, Shawn Rose, Ian Rosenfeldt, Russell Schneck, Russ Schoen, Troy Schubert, Pam Bochinski Simmeth, Stephanie Simon, Maura Sirena, Jenna Smith, Courtney Belluccio Sprague, Lauren St. George, Doug Stevenson, Randah Taher, Jon Tanzey, Panteli Tritchew, Taylor Upchurch, Marta Villanueva, Shawn Warnes, Emily White, Ayse Wiediger, Laszlo Wollner, John Yeo, MaryBeth Zacharias, Courtney Zwart

Our Twitter contributors include:

@BhargavPurohit, @danishbuddha, @dikwizdumbsvc, @FirstLazy, @gaudetj_99, @HughdjNicklin, @PanteliT, @Publishar, @QuartzCrystals, @ReMeij, @theezetster, @URC_Bob, @Vicaro, @visuele, @xraytext

# CONTENTS

# INTRODUCTION

Fostering creativity is an essential part of modern education. You probably agree, otherwise you wouldn't have picked up this book. But when did you reach this conclusion? Perhaps you watched Sir Ken Robinson's Ted talk[1] on creativity and schools, which inspired millions to think about education in new ways. Or maybe you have been reading up on 21st Century skills[2] and noticed their emphasis on problem solving, creativity, and innovation. Or perhaps you spend so much time teaching students the "correct" answers that you fear they might miss the opportunity to generate multiple solutions.

However you got here, there is a good chance that you want to bring creativity into your classroom. It's also likely that you, like the hundreds of teachers we have worked with, are now wrestling with three questions:

---

1   http://www.ted.com/talks/ken_robinson_says_schools_kill_creativity
2 http://www.p21.org/storage/documents/21st_century_skills_education_and_
competitiveness_guide.pdf

1. What exactly do we mean by creativity?
2. How do we foster creativity in the classroom?
3. How do we find enough time to fit it into the already crammed curriculum?

Fortunately, the purpose of this book is to give you solid, practical answers to all three questions. Our goal is to help you understand what creativity is, to show you how it can be integrated into your existing curriculum, and to help you do it without taking up additional classroom time. Let's get started with those questions.

## WHAT DO WE MEAN BY CREATIVITY?

Finding a definition of creativity isn't difficult. In fact, there are probably as many definitions as there are creativity researchers. And this isn't necessarily a bad thing. Trying to create a single definition, which can encompass everything from solving a mathematical problem in a new way, to cheering yourself up by painting your internal emotional state, is quite tricky. Clearly, creativity is a multifaceted subject, and the various definitions provide some insight into its nature.

And while there are many definitions, the research community has gradually moved toward one definition over the last fifty years, which has now become the de facto standard. This definition describes creativity as the "generation of novel and useful ideas."[3] It is a reasonable start, and it gives us a good way to think about the subject. However, as is usually the case with short, all-encompassing phrases, it misses a huge amount of what it means to be creative. It also doesn't necessarily help us understand what creativity looks like in a classroom.

Fortunately, E. Paul Torrance, who was known as the Father of Creativity[4] in education, did extensive research on the questions "What is creativity?" and "Is creativity teachable?"

3   Stein, M.I. (1974). Stimulating creativity. New York, NY: Academic Press.
4   Millar, G. W. (1995). E. Paul Torrance: The creativity man. Westport, CT: Praeger.

And, while his work is completely compatible with the standard definition, it provides us with a very different way of looking at the subject. Torrance and Safter's work identified a set of skills that children employ when they are being creative.[5] The beauty of these skills is that they help us to understand both how we could teach creativity, and what to look for to see if we are having an effect.

This book focuses on twelve of the skills that we believe are essential for creative teaching. The skills are:

- Produce and Consider Many Alternatives
- Enjoy and Use Fantasy
- Highlight the Essence
  Look at it Another Way
- Playfulness and Humor
- Be Original
- Be Aware of Emotions
- Put Ideas into Context
- Make it Swing! Make it Ring!
- Keep Open
- Get Glimpses of the Future
- Break Through and Extend the Boundaries

---

5  Torrance, E. P., & Safter, H. T. (1999). Making the creative leap beyond... Buffalo, NY: Creative Education Foundation Press.

Additionally, in our extensive experiences teaching creative problem solving, we have found the following four skills incredibly valuable in education:

- Curiosity
- Embrace the Challenge
- Mindfulness
- Tolerate the Ambiguity

These sixteen skills make up the foundation of what we believe is important for creativity in education.

## HOW DO YOU ORGANICALLY WEAVE THESE SKILLS INTO YOUR CLASSROOM WITHOUT USING UP ADDITIONAL TIME?

Once we had the sixteen creative thinking skills we felt were essential, we went out to schools, classes, and conferences and gathered ideas from educators all over the world on techniques and strategies to bring these skills into different types of classrooms. This resulted in a collaboration with over 150 educators generating over 800 ideas on how to deliberately incorporate these skills into education.

In each of the following chapters, you will find a description of the title skill, research to support it, many different ways to integrate the skill into your curriculum, language to enhance and encourage it, and tips to help you along the way.

Here is how we suggest you use this book: go through the chapters page by page, and put a Post-it next to the ideas you would like to try. Then, start with one that would be easy for you to implement. For example, perhaps you like the idea of having a curiosity corner in your classroom during Dr. Seuss week. Post a sign on top of a table and invite students to leave notes about all the things they are curious about in regards to Dr. Seuss! There are so many ideas that you can easily shift or adjust so they fit perfectly in your classroom.

Another strategy that we suggest is to find an existing lesson that isn't entirely engaging and to utilize one of the techniques to bring it to life! For example,

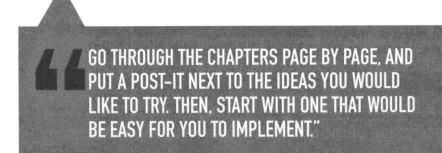

GO THROUGH THE CHAPTERS PAGE BY PAGE, AND PUT A POST-IT NEXT TO THE IDEAS YOU WOULD LIKE TO TRY. THEN, START WITH ONE THAT WOULD BE EASY FOR YOU TO IMPLEMENT."

imagine you have a relatively tedious lesson on railroad transportation. You might use the skill *Look at it Another Way*, and have the students think about the different ways they could transport something in comparison to a train! For example, what would it look like to have a pig in high heels transport your cargo?

Some of the ideas that you read may not be relevant to you. However, we ask that you keep open and let them spark your imagination! These ideas came from teachers, and they can easily be adjusted to fit your own curriculum.

Once you have tried these ideas, log on to our Facebook page[6] to find and share your experiences, and any more ideas that you may have come up with on your own! And don't forget to check out Creative Thinking for the Classroom,[7] an online course with short videos aimed at introducing and incorporating deliberate creative problem solving into your classroom!

6  https://www.facebook.com/WeavingCreativity
7  http://udemy.com/the-creative-thinking-course-for-teachers

# CURIOSITY

## HAVING A DESIRE TO DISCOVER, LEARN, OR KNOW.

Why is the sky blue? What makes the grass green? What does this button do? Our lives are built around the questions that we ask and the answers we discover. When we as humans don't understand something, our basic instincts tell us to figure it out. Over time, those instincts can be stifled or shunted off to the side – but why?

This skill is about reinforcing the internal urge to learn. And although learning is the central focus of classrooms and the educational system, curiosity itself could do with a lot more attention. Curiosity cultivates intrinsic motivation – the internal motivation that simply comes from the joy and interest of the task rather than external rewards. This leads to more driven and enjoyable learning within the classroom and without.

When students are naturally curious about the topic at

hand, they are more likely to learn more about it and remember the information longer.[8] Have you ever met a young child who could tell you everything about a brachiosaurus, simply because she had been curious enough to find out everything there was to know? Her curiosity, which is characteristic of all young children,[9] dwarfs that of adolescents and young adults.[10]

So how might we as teachers encourage that same curiosity in our students of all ages? The following ideas highlight some examples.

## TIPS FOR ENCOURAGING CURIOSITY IN THE CLASSROOM

1. Spend time asking open-ended questions, questions that do not have single answers.

2. Frequently ask your students what they are wondering about.

3. When students ask questions, don't rush to give them "the answer." First ask, "What do you think?"

---

8  Engel, S. (2009). Is curiosity vanishing? Journal of the American Academy of Child & Adolescent Psychiatry, 48(8), 777-779.
9  Bosse, S., Jacobs, G., & Anderson, T. L. (2009). Science in the air. Young Children, 64(6), 10-15.
10  Agosto, D. E., & Hughes-Hassell, S. (2005). People, places, and questions: An investigation of the everyday life information-seeking behaviors of urban young adults. Library & Information Science Research, 27(2), 141-163.

Often we focus on providing answers, but allowing students to think about their own questions can be very powerful.

4. Encourage your students to ask questions beyond the first "Why?"

5. Actively wonder about how your students perceive the world. When you can tap into your students' perspectives, you can understand them in a deeper way.

6. Be aware of the interests of your students and ask questions related to those interests.

7. Acknowledge the curiosity and questioning of your students. When a student asks an interesting question, say, "That's a great question!"

8. Avoid overstimulation. Sometimes when we focus on simplicity, curiosity knocks.

9. Post this list in your classroom: http://www. brainpickings.org/2012/08/24/how-to-be-an-explorer-of-the-world-keri-smith/

## QUICK IDEAS

10. Take an object related to the lesson, and keep it covered in the center of the room while you teach. Unveil it at the end of the lesson.

11. Create a class mascot related to creativity: Captain Curiosity, The Wondering Woman, etc.

12. Have students form their own "What if...?" questions to ask their classmates.

13. Give students magnifying glasses, binoculars, digital microscopes, etc. and have them explore things in the classroom.

14. Use the 5 Whys technique to answer tough questions: http://www.isixsigma.com/tools-templates/cause-effect/determine-root-cause-5-whys/

"GIVE STUDENTS MAGNIFYING GLASSES, BINOCULARS, DIGITAL MICROSCOPES, ETC. AND HAVE THEM EXPLORE THINGS IN THE CLASSROOM."

15. Provide students with a passage or a story and ask them to generate as many questions as they can about it.

16. When students ask a question, ask them where they might be able to find the answer – without using the internet!

17. When learning about how an object works, take the object apart together: an old cell phone, a hand mixer that doesn't work anymore, a broken vacuum cleaner, etc.

18. Ask students to break things open (a flower, seedpod, apple, pomegranate, geode, etc.), and be curious about what they discover.

19. Wonder together about the things you read in books. Learn about those things together. For example, a book with a bat character could lead to wondering and learning more about bats.

20. Explore different cultures. Be curious and learn about how different people live, play, dance, make music, etc.

21. Share the things that spark your own curiosity with your students.

22. Take out a map and wonder what it would be like to live in various parts of the world. Find ways (books, internet, old encyclopedias, etc.) to go on a visual adventure!

23. Encourage students to ask a question that you can't answer!

24. Go on a library hunt. Have students take a question and go hunt for answers in the library.

25. Have your students go through an old magazine and tear out pictures that they are curious about and like. Create a collage.

26. Go to http://wonderopolis.org/ and find out what the wonder of the day is. Share and discuss it with your students.

27. Start class with a YouTube clip that reflects the lesson.

28. Have a countdown ticker going at the start of class.

29. Ask students what they think they will know by the end of the semester.

30. Encourage students to look at a topic from a two-year-old's perspective, with a two-year-old's curiosity.

31. Before beginning any lesson, have students generate at least 20 questions that they have about the topic.

32. Ask students to come up with three unanswered questions after each lesson, and require them to look up the answers for homework.

33. Have students visit a public library and browse magazines on topics that they know little about.

34. Have students track how many questions they ask in a day – then challenge them to beat that number!

## EXTENDED IDEAS

35. Have a curiosity quotient: a number of curiosity questions to reach per day as a class.

36. Make a class wonder tree/wondering wall: a place to capture wonderings as they occur throughout the day.

37. Ask "What if...?" questions. What if we had four legs instead of two?" "What if there were no stores to buy food?" "What if the whole world was water and there was no land?"

38. Ask students to create Wonder journals, a place where they record questions that spark their curiosity.

39. Wonder, Think, Learn, Share. Have students identify something they wonder about. Then ask them to think of their own answers (the answers do not need to be correct). Then have them learn something about their wondering and share it with the class.

40. Go on a class curiosity adventure! These adventures can be elaborate field trips or a simple adventure down the hall. The key is having an adventurous attitude and intentionally allowing for curiosity and discovery to emerge. Try a curiosity adventure in your school neighborhood. Take a leisurely walk and allow your students to follow their curiosities. Walk slowly; really look, listen, touch, play, and explore.

41. Start a collection of interesting objects and bring an object out to explore on occasion. Provide the surprise of a new object to explore and spark curiosity. Allow your students time to explore the object, ask questions, discover, and have fun.

> **THE KEY IS HAVING AN ADVENTUROUS ATTITUDE AND INTENTIONALLY ALLOWING FOR CURIOSITY AND DISCOVERY TO EMERGE. TRY A CURIOSITY ADVENTURE IN YOUR SCHOOL NEIGHBORHOOD."**

42. Have a question day, and see how many questions your students can ask. Write them down and read them at the end of the day. Select a few to learn about and have your students share what they have learned with family at home.

43. Create a curiosity corner in your classroom. Make it a fun place for your students. As a class, put things in it that spark curiosity. Collect and display things from your curiosity adventures.

44. Give students a document to read with some of the words blanked out. Students should figure out what has been omitted.

45. Show students a very common object and ask them to think of as many questions about the object as they can.

46. Have a curiosity party, and celebrate all of the things that you and your students don't yet know but would like to learn about. Call it a "Yet Party!"

47. Give your students an exam where the answer is given, and the students must provide the question. The final grade can be based on how interesting and novel the questions are.

48. Ask students to spend an hour reading an encyclopedia and encourage them to follow links between entries. Have a class discussion on interesting finds and unexpected learning.

49. Create a mystery box and fill it with toys and objects of different size, shape, and texture. Have students reach in and choose one object to touch (but not remove). Ask the students, "What do you think this object smells like? What is its purpose? How might it taste? What could this object be?"

50. Repress your students' curiosity for a day. Do not allow questions, and do not allow students to look things up on their own. At the end of the day, discuss the importance of curiosity.

## LANGUAGE OF CURIOSITY

- The five questions- Who? What? Where? Why? How?
- I wonder...
- That is interesting!
- Wow! Look at that.
- Let's take a closer look.
- What do you notice?
- What do you think?
- What do you wonder?
- Let's explore it.
- Great question!
- Let's find out.
- You are so curious!
- What is that?
- Who is curious about this?
- I'm curious.

# DO YOU HAVE ANY MORE IDEAS ON WEAVING "CURIOSITY" INTO YOUR CURRICULUM? IF SO, WRITE THEM HERE!

# EMBRACE THE CHALLENGE

## TAKING ON CHALLENGES WITH A PROBLEM-SOLVING ATTITUDE.

What if you could look at every obstacle as an opportunity? What if each problem turned into an exercise in acceptance and open-mindedness? What if every situation could be turned into a chance for growth?

This skill is about developing an attitude of being open to challenges as opportunities for something new. In this day and age, most of us maintain the limiting viewpoint that all challenges equate to distressing problems. And while some challenges are frustrating, stressful, and annoying, it is important not to let that potential become a self-fulfilling prophecy. The key to Embracing the Challenge is to not become blocked by the stress of the situation, to keep thinking, and to view the challenge in a more productive way.

In general, this skill is a cornerstone for creative thinking. Studies have shown that keeping an open mind to challenges is directly connected to the ability to produce numerous and novel alternatives.[11][12] By incorporating this skill into everyday classroom activities and lessons, students will be more likely to increase their personal levels of creative performance.[13]

The following ideas highlight the incorporation of embracing challenges into a teaching curriculum.

## TIPS FOR EMBRACING THE CHALLENGE IN THE CLASSROOM

1. Use the word "challenge" often.

2. Help students identify challenges as they come up.

3. When students complain, make them phrase the complaint as a challenge statement. For example: "I don't like reading," can be changed to "How might I find things I like to read?" Use statement starters "How to..?" (H2?), "How might I..?" (HMI?), and "What might be all the..?" (WMBAT?)

4. Frame assignments as challenges.

11  McCrae, R.M. (1987). Creativity, divergent thinking, and openness to experience. Journal of Personality and Social Psychology, 52(6), 1258-1265.
12  Williams, S.D. (2004). Personality, attitude, and leader influences on divergent thinking and creativity in organizations. European Journal of Innovation Management, 7(3), 187-204.
13  George, J.M., & Zhou, J. (2001). When openness to experience and conscientiousness are related to creative behavior: An interactional approach. Journal of Applied Psychology, 86(3), 513-24.

5. Be willing to admit your own limitations and share with students how you overcome or compensate for those limitations.

6. Reward and focus on effort as well as success (see *Mindset* by Carol Dweck[14]).

7. Push students beyond their comfort zones. Help them to embrace being uncomfortable while at the same time keeping them safe.

8. Provide students with the needed scaffolding to work on challenges.

9. Make it fun: highlight the fun aspects of the challenge or encourage students to make the task more fun themselves.

10. Provide recognition for various aspects of

---

14  Dweck, C.S. (2007). Mindset: The new psychology of success. New York, NY: Ballantine Books.

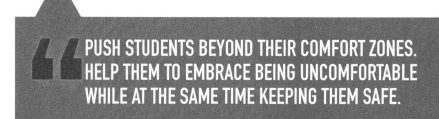

PUSH STUDENTS BEYOND THEIR COMFORT ZONES. HELP THEM TO EMBRACE BEING UNCOMFORTABLE WHILE AT THE SAME TIME KEEPING THEM SAFE.

embracing challenges: perseverance, risk taking, resourcefulness, achieving success, failing, making mistakes, etc.

11. Treat failures and mistakes as part of the road to success.

12. Eliminate unneeded criticism. Create an environment that is positive.

13. Remind students that there can be more than one right answer.

14. Find times to reward fluency (the ability to generate many ideas) vs. accuracy.

15. Stretch yourself and your students beyond the norm. A rubber band becomes useful when it is stretched – and so can your students when you push them beyond their comfort zones!

## QUICK IDEAS

16. Pose a weekly challenge to your students.

17. Explore the difference between a problem and a challenge.

18. Use riddles in the classroom.

19. Play challenging games that require cooperation and teamwork.

20. Give students challenging activities to do with their families or friends at home.

21. Share quotes about challenges and taking a positive attitude.

22. Give a weekly/monthly award or recognition to a student who demonstrates a problem-solving attitude. Ask students to nominate others.

23. Allow students to take a break from thinking about the challenge and do something hands-on that doesn't require much thought (doodling, playing with sculpting clay, etc.). Use this opportunity to teach students about the benefits of incubation.

24. Identify the parts of a challenge that are easy and parts that are more difficult.

25. Use a Game-ology approach. Turn classroom tasks, assignments, and challenges into games.

26. Look at big challenges and work with students to break them down into smaller challenges.

27. Help students to picture themselves on the other side of the challenge. What does successful completion of a challenge look like, and feel like?

28. Ask students to anonymously list what they want the outcomes of a challenge to be. Encourage them to think with no limitations.

29. Allow students to express fears and worries regarding the challenge. Use journaling or other ways of expression to address the emotional aspects of embracing challenges.

30. Have students draw the challenge.

31. Take one problem and work on it as a team. Can we brainstorm ways to overcome this challenge?

32. Have students think about how their education will ultimately change the world.

33. Allow opportunities for students to apply their knowledge to a hobby, or to other interests.

34. Bring the challenge back to their passions. How does the challenge connect to things that the students love? How might they use what they love to channel their passions?

35. Examine why a task is hard. Help students to articulate the challenges associated with the task.

36. Allow students to re-introduce the challenge, stating the challenge in their own words.

37. Have the students act out the challenge.

38. Require the students to fail a challenge or task, or identify ways they could fail.

39. Introduce students to quotes about challenges such as, "Rome wasn't built in a day," "Genius in 10% inspiration and 90% perspiration," or "Nothing great was ever achieved without enthusiasm."

40. Have a wall of famous people and ideas that once failed.

41. Challenge students to create a game based on class topics or for review.

42. Ask students to research other people who have overcome similar challenges.

43. Challenge students to prove you wrong.

44. Invite students to invent something that would make a problem less challenging.

45. Encourage students to share how they solved a problem.

46. Ask students to identify what might be the most difficult part of a project, paper, or assignment.

## EXTENDED IDEAS

47. Remove the pressure of a grade/credit associated with the challenge. Begin new concepts "grade-free" and gradually add grade-valued assessments.

48. Pose a learning challenge at the beginning of the year, such as: learn to juggle, do a magic trick, eat with chopsticks, or solve a Rubik's Cube. Then have a celebration at the end of the year where students can show what they learned to do.

49. Create a way for students to work on solving a problem in conjunction with other students across the world.

50. Challenge students to use sketches or Mind Maps (see http://www.mindtools.com/pages/article/newISS_01.htm) to illustrate problems, processes, and/or understandings of a topic.

## LANGUAGE OF EMBRACING THE CHALLENGE

- This is a challenge.
- It looks like a challenge.
- I have a challenge for you.
- You are working on a challenge.
- Let's think about it.
- Let's take a breath and look at it again.
- I am frustrated.
- You look frustrated.
- This is a fun challenge.
- What ideas do you have?
- How could we...?
- How to...?
- What might be all the ways we could...?
- How might we...?
- In what ways could we...?

## DO YOU HAVE ANY MORE IDEAS ON WEAVING "EMBRACE THE CHALLENGE" INTO YOUR CURRICULUM? IF SO, WRITE THEM HERE!

# PRODUCE AND CONSIDER MANY ALTERNATIVES

## GENERATING MANY AND VARIED IDEAS OR OPTIONS.

Have you ever needed to come up with a solution to a problem, jumped on the first answer that popped into your head, and proceeded to put it into action? Has it always worked out for you? More likely than not, this wasn't the best solution for the problem at hand, but it seemed like a good idea at the time.

This skill is about going beyond the obvious and producing a variety of possible solutions, ideas, or options. When we produce and consider multiple alternatives, we are more likely to have more viable, successful solutions.[15] However, as we mature, our ability to produce many alternatives seems to fade. Between Kindergarten and second grade students alone, there is a 74% drop in creativity rankings.[16] We as teachers are responsible for keeping this skill alive.

---

15  Torrance, E.P., & Safter, H. T. (1999). Making the Creative Leap Beyond... Buffalo, NY: Creative Education Foundation Press.
16  McGarvey, R. (1990). Creative thinking. USAIR, 36

The act of producing many alternatives is known as divergent thinking. In order to excel at divergence, one must be able to defer judgment, strive for quantity, make connections, and seek novelty.[17] Deferring judgment, or temporarily suspending evaluation of ideas and options as they are being generated, is the chief principle of divergence. Striving for quantity is the ability to produce many alternatives. It's what great creators do: they are fluent thinkers who generate many possibilities when faced with a problem. Making connections encourages building off of one another's ideas or borrowing ideas from other fields and areas of study, and seeking novelty urges the generation of original, wacky, or innovative options. These guidelines are key when it comes to divergent thinking and the tools that support it – including the ever-popular Brainstorming tool.

The following ideas highlight the incorporation of producing and considering many alternatives into a teaching curriculum.

---

17  Osborn, A.F. (1957). Applied imagination. New York, NY: Scribner.

## TIPS FOR PRODUCING AND CONSIDERING MANY ALTERNATIVES IN THE CLASSROOM

1. Design a single lesson in more than one way.

2. Explore the many different ways of learning something with your students.

3. Give a prize for the most ideas.

4. Engage in "What If..." thinking.

5. Provide a variety of materials to experiment with - cutting, tearing, etc.

6. As a teacher, produce many alternatives to questions and challenges. This will encourage your students to do the same!

## QUICK IDEAS

7. Ask students to think of many different ways they could explain a class topic to another person.

8. Challenge students to write as many words as they can with the letters in their full name.

9. Teach students about divergent thinking: http://bit.ly/divergentthinkinglesson

10. Present different forms of music.

11. Practice brainstorming activities with your class. (What might be all the uses for duct tape? What would make up the perfect classroom?)

12. Work in groups to redefine the problem.

13. When reading a passage, choose different words to emphasize in order to show how it can change the meaning of the text.

14. Use Mad Libs, or have students create their own.

15. Teach students about Brainstorming with Post-it notes. Each student writes their ideas on Post-it notes – one idea per Post-it – and sticks them up on the wall.

16. Ask students, "What are all the ways you could represent _____ (a cup, a bird, etc.)?"

17. Study the title of a piece of writing. Ask students to think about what the article/story could be about.

18. Ask students to come up with fifty titles to represent a story.

19. Have students list or draw out possible connections to a concept or topic.

20. Stop reading a story at the climax and list all the possible conclusions.

21. Have students tell a story back and forth across two groups.

22. Teach students how to Mind Map: http://www.mindtools.com/pages/article/newISS_01.htm

23. Use experiential learning where students can test their hypotheses by considering many alternatives.

24. Challenge students to make class content wearable.

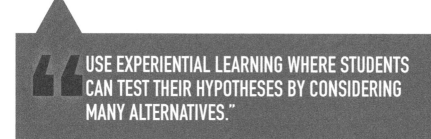

USE EXPERIENTIAL LEARNING WHERE STUDENTS CAN TEST THEIR HYPOTHESES BY CONSIDERING MANY ALTERNATIVES."

25. Have students think of a variety of different strategies for studying for their exams.

26. Ask students, "What is half of 8?" Encourage many answers by responding, "Yes, and...?"

27. Ask students, "What are all the ways to make 4?" If they get stumped after giving mathematical answers, offer answers such as "by holding up four fingers" and so on.

28. Pose the challenge to students to think of as many uses or improvements as they can for a: Q-tip, paperclip, brick, pair of tongs, chopsticks, water bottle, etc.

29. Ask your question in many different ways: "What is an obvious answer?" "What is a sneaky answer?" "What is a quick answer?" "What is a complicated answer?"

30. Teach students how to do a Word Dance: http://creativeproblemsolving.com/tools/worddance_worksheet.pdf

31. Play different versions of the same song. Encourage students to think about the instruments that could be used to make the song different.

32. Draw a shape or line and have students make different pictures starting with that shape.

33. Have students design several different sketches or prototypes for a logo.

34. Explore and replicate forms and processes found in nature.

35. Have students choose a favorite food, then prepare and eat it in a variety of ways (i.e. bananas can be peeled from the top or bottom, sliced into circles or strips, mashed up, made into smoothies, pudding, muffins, bread, etc.).

36. Have students come up with different ways to say happy birthday to someone (i.e. with a present, with a hug, with the birthday song, etc.)

37. Ask, "What might be all the ways to get from one place to another?"

## EXTENDED IDEAS

38. Give students some supplies (rubber band, ball, newspaper, tape, paper cup, straw, etc.) and have them create a variety of games using only the available materials.

39. Have students practice Brainstorming while following the guidelines for divergent thinking: http://bit.ly/brainstorminglesson

40. Have students design a variety of experiments to test a hypothesis.

41. Challenge students to find other solutions to problems that are already solved.

42. Ask, and encourage students to ask, BIG questions that have no known answer. Then come up with a variety of potential answers.

43. Choose a recurring problem in your classroom and ask students to generate many different ideas to overcome this problem.

44. Ask students to consider their hands (or other simple objects), and come up with as many different additions or modifications for them as possible.

45. Give students a "Once upon a time there was a _____" start and have them finish the story one after another.

46. Use an Idea Box as a way to generate stories. Have a column for characters, settings, plots, etc., and pick a random cell from each column to create a new story.

47. Have students write multiple endings to a paper they are writing.

48. Have students use Forced Connections to produce more ideas: https://brooklynbilbao.wordpress.com/2011/08/02/forced-connections/

49. Introduce SCAMPER as a tool for coming up with more ideas: http://www.creativeadvantage.com/scamper.html

50. Have students generate a list of people they would want in the room to help them solve a challenge. Ask students to list ideas that those individuals might have.

" USE AN IDEA BOX AS A WAY TO GENERATE STORIES. HAVE A COLUMN FOR CHARACTERS, SETTINGS, PLOTS, ETC., AND PICK A RANDOM CELL FROM EACH COLUMN TO CREATE A NEW STORY. "

## LANGUAGE OF PRODUCING AND CONSIDERING MANY ALTERNATIVES

- What could this be?
- This could be...
- What if...?
- What else...?
- How else..?.
- Where else...?
- Who else...?
- Why do you think...?
- Let's try it a different way.
- What might be all the ways...?

## DO YOU HAVE ANY MORE IDEAS ON WEAVING "PRODUCE AND CONSIDER MANY ALTERNATIVES" INTO YOUR CURRICULUM? IF SO, WRITE THEM HERE!

# ENJOY **AND** USE FANTASY

## IMAGINE, PLAY AND CONSIDER THINGS THAT ARE NOT CONCRETE OR DO NOT YET EXIST.

magine you've been given access to the world's first time machine. As of right now, it only has one setting: to take you on a journey 1000 years forward in time. Just think! You will be the first person from the present to see what the future looks like: what people will be wearing, what businesses will be in place, what governments will be standing, and the effects of the human race on the entire planet. With 100% assurance that the time machine is 100% safe, you hop in and press the One Button: GO!

This skill is all about imagination, and is an integral part of creativity and learning. The ability to enjoy and use fantasy is a skill that can be applied to many facets in life. Though it is often misconstrued as inconvenient or inappropriate (especially as students get older), fantasy has been shown to motivate learning in children while providing a non-threatening environment. When teachers employ fantasy and imagination in the classroom, their students' academic experiences are vastly improved, as are their thinking, logic, and communication skills. [18] (And we're willing to bet that the teachers have better experiences, too!)

With the proper balance of fantasy and imagination in a classroom setting, this skill not only encourages creativity, it also nurtures emotional and intellectual growth.[19] This is true in primary schools and beyond – evidence shows that the use of fantasy in the classroom environment is beneficial to students from kindergarten all the way through the graduate level of teaching and learning. Other studies support the idea that fantasy can inspire intrinsic motivation and interest, two characteristics that are commonly valued in the classroom.[20] By exploring different fantasy strategies, children are more likely to retain the "tested" information that they are required to learn. And the best part about using fantasy as a teaching tool? It's engaging, intriguing, and fun!

The following ideas highlight the incorporation of imagination and play into a teaching curriculum, along with the consideration of things that are not concrete or do not yet exist.

18   Osherson, S. (2004). The teacher's tin cup: Engaging fantasy and feeling in the classroom. Schools: Studies in Education, 1(2), p. 75-88.
19   Smith, M. & Mathur, R. (2009). Children's imagination and fantasy: Implications for development, education, and classroom activities. Research in the Schools, 16(1), p. 52-63.
20   Bergin, D. A. (2010). Influences on classroom interest. Educational Psychologist, 34(2), p. 87-98.

## TIPS FOR ENJOYING AND USING FANTASY IN THE CLASSROOM

1. Encourage students to use fantasy to solve real present day challenges.

2. Incorporate the fantasy genre into reading assignments. (*The Lord of the Rings, Harry Potter, The Hunger Games*, etc.)

3. Ask "What If" questions.

## QUICK IDEAS

4. Ask, "What could be all of the applications of teleportation technology?"

5. As a class, explore what life would be like with less gravity.

6. Encourage students to visualize what could go wrong in different scenarios, such as failure to follow safety procedures.

7. Ask students, "Imagine that you had a time machine. Where would you go in your time machine? Why would you go to this time and place?"

8. Have students imagine having hands that could turn into whatever items they needed at the moment.

9. Watch old Science Fiction videos and TV shows in class and see what has actually been invented.

10. Ask students, "How could you design a self-cleaning refrigerator?"

11. Help students to identify and think of ways to remove barriers that are known to exist.

12. Have students create a list of "Wouldn't It Be Great If...(WIBGI) statements.

13. Give an assignment that flips the gender roles.

14. Ask students to imagine the world 100 years ago.

15. Have students imagine that there was no fresh water available. What might be all the things that could happen?

16. Add a verse to "Jabberwocky" as a class.

17. Ask students to imagine how the classroom would look if they were giants or ants.

18. Speak in Pig Latin to your class.

19. Use role-playing in the classroom.

20. Ask students, "What could an alien world look like?"

21. Bring an object in and ask students what it might become.

22. Tell a story from the perspective of the murder weapon.

23. Explore class topics through cartoon characters.

24. Ask, "What superpowers would you want to have?" Have students create a superhero based on these powers.

25. Invite students to physically act out cellular movement, waveforms, and other scientific concepts.

26. Introduce students to Sim City, and encourage them to build and destroy cities in interesting ways.

27. Explore Biomimicry, the study and mimicry of how nature solves problems. Integrate nature and innovation. How could humans use the abilities of different animals and plants?

28. Pose the question, "What would you do with a time extender device?"

29. Ask students, "If you had to make up your own word, what would it be and what would it mean?"

## EXTENDED IDEAS

30. Have students imagine, write, or act out a conversation with a historical person.

31. Have students put themselves into a scene of the book they are reading, or into a historical event.

32. Ask students to imagine that the earth was made of non-Newtonian fluid, AKA Oobleck. Think about how we would live. What would our houses be like? How could we grow food? How could we get around?

33. Have students think of scenarios through role reversal, i.e. role reversal in a colonization scenario.

34. Ask students, "Imagine that you could travel through time and change one historical event. What would you change? How would you change it? What would the effects of the change be?"

35. Have students write a familiar story in a fantasy setting.

36. Give students opportunities to animate class topics or concepts.

37. Give students an assignment that makes them think about the application of class topics to a new business venture.

38. Have students create comic strips, movie scripts, visual representations, tools, inventions, or games based on class topics or concepts.

39. Have students build comic books with heroes and abilities that students want, but don't have.

40. Have students take a familiar story and create a new ending, setting, character, etc.

41. Challenge students to create a film based on class concepts.

42. Invent a new alphabet system and write a message to the class.

43. Ask, "If you could travel anywhere to study, where would you go and what would you study?" Try to incorporate their answers in your lessons.

44. Encourage students to research dreams and daydreaming.

45. Have students create commercials for research.

46. Create a new language - by combining root words, prefixes, and suffixes, then "define" the words.

47. Have students explore Second Life (http://secondlife.com/) or McLarin's Adventures (http://dgbl.ou.edu/mclarin/).

48. Have students change all of the main characters in a book into animals. How does the major conflict change?

49. Have students take a historical event and turn it into a nursery rhyme.

50. Ask students, "If you could publish a book, what would it be about? If you could run a publication/press, what kinds of authors, works would you publish?"

## LANGUAGE FOR ENJOYING AND USING FANTASY

- Imagine that...
- Let's pretend.
- Let's imagine...

## DO YOU HAVE ANY MORE IDEAS ON WEAVING "ENJOY AND USE FANTASY" INTO YOUR CURRICULUM? IF SO, WRITE THEM HERE!

# HIGHLIGHT THE ESSENCE

## IDENTIFYING WHAT IS MOST IMPORTANT AND ABSOLUTELY ESSENTIAL.

Have you ever been working on a problem and suddenly found yourself completely sidetracked? Perhaps you began to focus on one aspect of the situation that was easy to solve, but not the actual problem. Though you may have felt productive for an instant, having solved that small issue, the overall problem had not been taken care of. All of this could have been avoided had you simply highlighted the essence of the situation.

This skill is about identifying that which is most important or essential in any given situation. The thinking involved in this process is required in many aspects of creative expressiveness and problem solving,[21] and it is recognized as one of the primary traits of creative individuals.[22] By

21  Torrance, E.P., & Safter, H. T. (1999). Making the Creative Leap Beyond... Buffalo, NY: Creative Education Foundation Press.
22  Aboukinane, C. (2007). A qualitative study of creative thinking using experiential learning in an agriculture and life sciences course (Unpublished doctoral dissertation). Texas A&M University, College Station, Texas.

helping them to distinguish between relevant and irrelevant material, students will be more capable problem solvers.

The following ideas promote the incorporation of highlighting the essence into a teaching curriculum.

## TIPS FOR HIGHLIGHTING THE ESSENCE IN THE CLASSROOM

1. Use color-coding in lessons and activities to help with visualization and matching.

2. Introduce students to the Popplet app (http://popplet.com/) for collaborative concept-mapping.

3. Have plenty of highlighters handy.

## QUICK IDEAS

4. At the end of each class, have students write a short "What was the point?" response to the lesson.

5. When reading, ask students to think about what the author's goal may have been.

6. Ask students to pick a song that reminds them of a class topic or concept.

7. Ask students, "In 10 words or less, what is one thing you learned today?"

8. Play the "Telephone Game" with pithy passages.

9. Ask students, "What color represents your thoughts on _____, and why?"

10. Make a poster based on a class topic or concept.

11. Challenge students to create a comic strip in one frame based on class topics or concepts.

12. Have students write a Tweet (140 characters or less) to highlight what they have learned.

13. Find a picture that symbolizes class concepts.

14. Have students make a cheat sheet.

15. Have students create test questions.

16. Challenge students to write a Haiku. Try exploring the Haiku Deck App.

17. Ask students to give a 30 second overview or elevator pitch.

18. Have students create a message in a bottle.

19. Play "Find the core." Discuss how to dig down and uncover the root of a concept or a story.

20. Challenge students to create their own shorthand for note taking.

21. Have students create newspaper headlines related to lessons.

22. Have students write down one key takeaway after each lesson.

23. Imitate an author's tone in made-up one-liners.

24. Have students make an outline.

25. Encourage students to find an image, product or single item that represents the story.

26. Have students write main ideas on Post-it notes.

27. Let students draw a picture.

28. Have students write an abstract.

29. Create a flowchart of the primary concept and its building blocks.

30. Have students highlight the most important words in a short piece. Then put those words in a list or a poem or a new sentence.

31. Have students explain the essence of what they have learned in 3 minutes to a peer.

32. Challenge students to explain "entrepreneurship" (or a different term) in a few words to other students.

33. Have students write a review in a descending countdown using 16 words, eight words, four words, two words.

## EXTENDED IDEAS

34. Have students identify common aspects within a set of diverse processes.

35. Challenge students to make a video to teach a process or concept in 1 minute or less.

36. Have students write a blog based on class topics or concepts.

37. Challenge students to create Rap lyrics about the lesson.

38. Have students design a study guide or review game for an exam.

39. Challenge students to create a way to explain a class concept to a 3-year-old.

40. Have students make a one-minute commercial about a class topic.

41. For homework, have students send a text message to someone highlighting the essence of a lesson.

42. Have students read a story and retell it in 6 sentences or less.

43. Challenge students to make short presentations.

44. Sort the class into teams. Each team has to pick three key words that they feel represents the essence of a passage - ask them to debate and defend their choice to other teams.

45. Challenge students to create a video shot in one frame.

46. Have students create a travel brochure to a place or location that is being studied.

47. Challenge students to write a six-word synopsis of a class concept or lesson.

48. Have students develop a guide for future students about how to be successful in school or how to avoid pitfalls.

49. Ask students to write a children's book that simplifies a difficult concept.

50. Challenge students to draw a postage stamp representing the theme of each chapter.

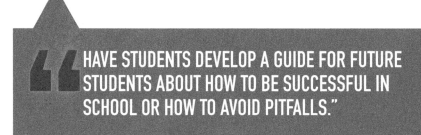

HAVE STUDENTS DEVELOP A GUIDE FOR FUTURE STUDENTS ABOUT HOW TO BE SUCCESSFUL IN SCHOOL OR HOW TO AVOID PITFALLS."

## LANGUAGE OF HIGHLIGHTING THE ESSENCE

- Keep it short and simple.
- Let's summarize this.
- Highlight what is most important.

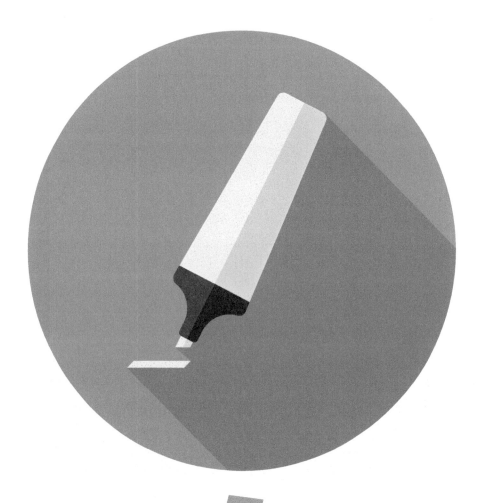

# DO YOU HAVE ANY MORE IDEAS ON WEAVING "HIGHLIGHT THE ESSENCE" INTO YOUR CURRICULUM? IF SO, WRITE THEM HERE!

........................................................................

........................................................................

........................................................................

........................................................................

........................................................................

........................................................................

........................................................................

........................................................................

........................................................................

........................................................................

........................................................................

# LOOK AT IT **ANOTHER** WAY

## PERCEIVING THINGS FROM DIFFERENT PERSPECTIVES.

What if *Harry Potter* had been written about a girl? What would she be called? How would that change the central relationships – would she have the same friends and enemies? How would she have tackled the same issues? Would the author's tone have changed, and if so, how?

This skill is about seeing things from multiple perspectives, views, or mindsets. The ability to shift the way we look at things is integral to maintaining a quick and creative mind, when it comes to both solving problems and approaching novel situations.[23] This is especially important if we want to teach our students how to break out of routine and generate new approaches and patterns, two skills that are highly attractive in this day and age.[24] [25]

---

23  Torrance, E.P., & Safter, H. T. (1999). Making the Creative Leap Beyond... Buffalo, NY: Creative Education Foundation Press.
24  de Bono, E. (1970). Lateral thinking: A textbook of creativity. London, UK: Penguin.
25  de Bono, E. (1995). Serious creativity. The Journal of Quality and Participation, 18(5), 12-18.

The following ideas highlight the incorporation of different perspectives into a teaching curriculum.

## TIPS FOR LOOKING AT IT ANOTHER WAY IN THE CLASSROOM

1. Use your garbage for lesson plans.

2. Ask "What if..." questions.

3. Compare keywords in content from different fields.

## QUICK IDEAS

4. Teach a lesson using no words, then assign the same task to your students.

5. Make students act something out – the life cycle of a plant, a scene in a book, etc.

6. Have students write alternate endings.

7. Give students a solution and have them work backward to uncover the many problems that might lead to the solution.

8. Ask students to build something out of non-traditional materials.

9. Challenge students to turn one thing into something different.

10. Have students use different mediums to express the same ideas.

11. Ask students to retell the story in another genre.

12. Have students switch partners.

13. Read in different voices for each character.

14. Use props to teach concepts and topics.

15. Play *Jeopardy!* with the students - provide the answers and ask them to generate the questions.

16. Have students consider how they wish their classes were taught. Ask students to teach a topic to the class in a way that they would like to have it taught to them.

17. Change the gender of a character.

18. Have students stand on top of their chairs or sit under desks to gain a new perspective or to look at a problem in another way.

19. Ask students to look at a situation from a family member's perspective.

20. Tell both sides of a story.

21. Have students tell someone else's story.

22. Adopt the lens of a different discipline.

23. Ask students, "What ideas would _____ have for this?" (i.e. Mickey Mouse, an astronaut, the president, a 5-year-old, etc.)

24. Have students look at a class topic from the teacher's perspective.

25. Choose another protagonist for a story.

26. Have someone else lead the conversation/share the message.

27. Look at different prototypes of the same thing.

28. Encourage students to put themselves in a character's shoes.

29. Examine different problems that use the same solution.

30. Ask, "How would a bug see this?"

31. Change the way the room is set up, and ask your students how it feels to sit in different parts of the room.

32. Think about how you would teach if you could use no technology.

33. Have students take photographs of a "subject" from around the room.

34. Have class on the playground.

35. Play the game "Another Way to Say": when opportunities arise, share other words that mean the same thing.

## EXTENDED IDEAS

36. Look at teaching from the point of view of students, administration, and parents.

37. Design or teach a lesson backward.

38. Explore how other cultures teach students.

39. Have students create and wear different glasses and ask them what they see.

40. Give students a problem to solve, such as homelessness. Have them look at the problem from all different perspectives. What does each constituent see and experience?

41. Explore information about different ethnicities and cultures.

42. Have students view multiple versions of a scene, and then create different versions of a different scene.

43. Have students create videos from their perspectives.

44. Switch theoretical perspectives – have students defend a point of view that they don't agree with, and see how their perspectives change.

45. Have students take photo portraits of their friends and capture them at different angles.

46. In Art, ask everyone to view and draw an object, then compare how it is different from different points of view.

47. Give students the opportunity to process lesson plans and information in a different environment.

48. Change the light in the classroom.

49. Give students an opportunity to shadow a professional in unfamiliar areas.

50. Have your class "adopt" a flower, plant or tree on your school ground. Take a photograph of the plant on the same day each month. What does it look like as it changes through each season? Post the photographs in the room.

> HAVE YOUR CLASS "ADOPT" A FLOWER, PLANT OR TREE ON YOUR SCHOOL GROUND. TAKE A PHOTOGRAPH OF THE PLANT ON THE SAME DAY EACH MONTH. WHAT DOES IT LOOK LIKE AS IT CHANGES THROUGH EACH SEASON? POST THE PHOTOGRAPHS IN THE ROOM."

## LANGUAGE OF LOOKING AT IT IN ANOTHER WAY

- Let's look at it differently.
- Turn it upside down.
- Let's get another perspective.
- I never thought of it that way.
- Change your perspective for a moment.

## DO YOU HAVE ANY MORE IDEAS ON WEAVING "LOOK AT IT ANOTHER WAY" INTO YOUR CURRICULUM? IF SO, WRITE THEM HERE!

# MINDFULNESS

## BEING IN THE PRESENT MOMENT.

S it in a place and position where you feel comfortable. Relax your breathing and clear your mind. Think about what you are doing right now – reading this book, and perhaps drinking coffee or snacking on peanuts. What do you hear? What do you smell? What do you taste, and feel, and see?

Mindfulness is about being fully immersed in the present moment. It is about being open and aware, while experiencing with all of our senses. When we are mindful, we are focused on the present moment, and allowing it to unfold its possibilities. And this can lead to a more creative classroom.

Being mindful and encouraging mindfulness in your students induces a state of mind that encourages the production of numerous and novel ideas.[26] Though there are those who believe that mindfulness and meditation

---

26  Colzato, L.S., Ozturk, A., & Hommel, B. (2012). Meditate to create: The impact of focused-attention and open-monitoring training on convergent and divergent thinking. Frontiers in Psychology, 3:116.

lead to daydreaming, studies have shown that practicing mindfulness encourages stronger attention-regulation and executive functioning, two skills that are key in productive students. [27] [28] [29] [30] Ultimately, using mindfulness in the classroom is incredibly beneficial to the students, both academically and socially.[31]

The following ideas highlight the incorporation of mindfulness into a teaching curriculum.

## TIPS FOR ENCOURAGING MINDFULNESS IN THE CLASSROOM

1. Teach students to be in the present moment and to focus on the task at hand.

2. Help students develop reflective thinking. Give them time for reflection.

3. Utilize the physical space intentionally, re-arranging the environment so that it supports the task at hand.

27  Heeren A., Van Broeck N., Philippot P. (2009). The effects of mindfulness on executive processes and autobiographical memory specificity. Behaviour Research and Therapy, 47(5), 403–409.
28  Jha A. P., Krompinger J., Baime M. J. (2007). Mindfulness meditation modifies subsystems of attention. Cognitive, Affective, & Behavioral Neuroscience, 7(2), 109–119.
29  Moore A., Malinowski P. (2009). Meditation, mindfulness and cognitive flexibility. Consciousness & Cognition, 18(1), 176–186.
30  Zeidan F., Johnson S. K., Diamond B. J., David Z., Goolkasian P. (2010). Mindfulness meditation improves cognition: evidence of brief mental training. Consciousness & Cognition, 19(2), 597–605.
31  Zelazo, P.D., & Lyons, K.E. (2012). The potential benefits of mindfulness training in early childhood: A developmental social cognitive neuroscience perspective. Child Development Perspectives, 6(2), 154-160.

4. Remove distractions.

5. Set the tone and mood of the lesson with physical stimuli.

6. Encourage students to get away from phones and technology.

7. Allow students and teachers to slow down the process.

8. Encourage students to make observations throughout the day.

9. Give students more time to consider problems and situations.

10. Get students out of their desks.

11. Help students learn to visualize.

12. Give students more choices.

## QUICK IDEAS

13. Teach observation skills – incorporate all five senses into your lessons.

14. Have students trace items on paper – slowly and silently.

15. Lead students through a guided relaxation.

16. Lead students in a progressive muscle relaxation.

17. Have students sit and do nothing.

18. Teach diaphragmatic breathing.

19. Encourage students to establish an awareness of the physical space.

20. Teach students about active listening. What does it mean to be a good listener? How can you tell when someone is listening to you? Have students practice listening to a classmate without distraction.

21. Ask students to silently walk around the room and write down things that they notice for the first time.

22. Sit in silence as a class and listen to the breath of the room.

23. Make students multitask and discuss how it feels. Then give them a mindful task, and ask how that feels. Compare the two experiences.

24. Turn off the lights and read a story to the students.

25. Slow down the experience by using moments of silence and allowing quiet moments to happen.

26. Play I Spy.

27. Have students reflect on how their semester is going and have others respond to these issues.

28. Show students a picture related to the lesson. Ask them to spend some time looking at the details and describing what they see.

29. Ask students to write down detailed steps for an action that is usually performed on autopilot (i.e. brushing teeth, driving to work, etc.).

30. Have students close their eyes and answer questions about the classroom around them.

31. Take your class for a walk and ask them to be observant of what they see.

32. Have students mindfully explain a concept to another student.

33. Teach students to pause each day and look at the sky.

## EXTENDED IDEAS

34. Have a lesson where students mindfully eat something. For example, have a candy-tasting experience (allergies permitting). Have students focus on a piece of candy, smell it, touch it, look deeply at it, and taste it. Then have them try that with the content they are working on.

35. Encourage students to develop an awareness of the cultural relevance of a lesson.

36. Have students go outside, close their eyes, and draw a picture of what they hear.

37. Ask students to experience a normal daily activity with mindfulness (washing hands, eating, walking to the bus, being with a pet, etc.). Then have students write about their experiences. Ask what they noticed and felt, and how it was different from the other times they had done this activity.

38. Start the day/week with a quote and ask the students to think about what it means to them.

39. Take some time at the beginning of the day to focus as a class, to let go of anything that is bothering them and set the intention for the day.

40. Take some time at the end of the day to have each student share one thing that happened during the day for which he or she is grateful.

41. Ask students to write or draw in journals.

42. Have students engage in descriptive writing using their five senses.

43. Create a class observation notebook.

44. Have students draw a still life. Do not grade the final product – instead, discuss the process of slowing down and noticing different aspects of the subject.

45. Have a day of easy yoga.

46. Use "See, Think, Wonder" – present an art piece (or any object) and have students write what they see, what ideas it sparks, and what questions spring out of those thoughts.

47. Give students a chart with five columns – one for each sense. Have them cross off "sight" and fill in the other four columns with things they experience throughout the day.

48. Challenge students to write a five-line, five-senses riddle, describing something without naming it. Can others guess the answer?

49. Give each student a plant seed or sprout to nurture. Have students write down observations of the plants' developments.

50. Ask students to take "mental pictures" of specific lesson moments that they would like to remember.

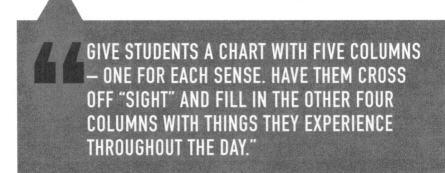

GIVE STUDENTS A CHART WITH FIVE COLUMNS – ONE FOR EACH SENSE. HAVE THEM CROSS OFF "SIGHT" AND FILL IN THE OTHER FOUR COLUMNS WITH THINGS THEY EXPERIENCE THROUGHOUT THE DAY."

## LANGUAGE OF MINDFULNESS

- What do you notice?
- What do you hear?
- What do you see?
- How does it feel?
- Let's focus.
- Be still.
- Listen carefully.
- Enjoy what you are doing.
- Describe what you are doing.
- Slow down.
- Stop and smell the roses.
- Pay attention.

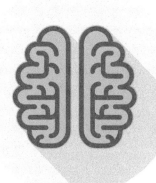
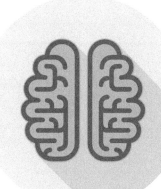

## DO YOU HAVE ANY MORE IDEAS ON WEAVING "MINDFULNESS" INTO YOUR CURRICULUM? IF SO, WRITE THEM HERE!

# PLAYFULNESS **AND** HUMOR

## FREELY TOYING WITH IDEAS.

**W**hat was your favorite game to play as a child? Duck, duck, goose? Hide and seek? Or did you prefer telling knock-knock jokes? As children, playing and humor come naturally to us. But along the journey of life, we often set aside the fun in order to focus on more "important" things.

This skill is about bringing fun, playfulness, and humor back into the classroom. Play is a powerhouse. It provides physical, mental, emotional and social benefits for students and teachers alike. When it comes to creative thinking, playfulness allows us to engage in imagination; explore and toy with thoughts, ideas, and possibilities; have a more optimistic perspective; harness intrinsic motivation; make mistakes and bounce back; and engage in problem solving.

Playfulness and humor are essential skills in everyday life, and they are especially important in the classroom. In fact, both playfulness and humor have proven to be predictors of creativity and sociability in students.[32] [33] [34]

The following ideas highlight the incorporation of playfulness and humor into a teaching curriculum.

## TIPS FOR ENCOURAGING PLAYFULNESS AND HUMOR IN THE CLASSROOM

1. Be willing to show your silly side.

2. Don't be afraid to laugh in class.

3. Give yourself permission to be childlike.

## QUICK IDEAS

4. Teach class with a clown nose or other silly variation.

5. Sing to your students while handing out items, making up lyrics about the lesson from a familiar song.

6. Ask illogical questions to get students to prove to themselves that they understand the material.

---

32 Chang, C.P. (2013). Relationship between playfulness and creativity among students gifted in mathematics and science. Creative Education, 4(2), 101-109.
33 Ghayas, S., & Malik, F. (2013). Sense of humor as a predictor of creativity level in university undergraduates. Journal of Behavioural Sciences, 23(2).
34 Ziv, A., & Gadish, O. (1989). Humor and marital satisfaction. Journal of Social Psychology, 129(6), 759-768

7.  Take a break and teach students to juggle with scarves.

8.  Toss a ball, soft toy, or a rubber chicken while moving from speaker to speaker.

9.  Create a new holiday (i.e. Sprinkle Day, Colorful Socks Day, Porcupine Day, etc.).

10. Create a silly name for the day.

11. Have students create code names.

12. As a class, create a riddle or limerick based on a class topic or concept.

13. Let students in on an "inside joke."

14. Ask students for the wrong answer first.

15. Play charades with class concepts and topics.

16. Create a humorous "instructional" video.

CREATE A NEW HOLIDAY (I.E. SPRINKLE DAY, COLORFUL SOCKS DAY, PORCUPINE DAY, ETC.).

17. Incorporate improv into your lessons.

18. Watch Charlie Chaplin and Three Stooges comedies.

19. Break out in dance in the middle of class.

20. Communicate in jumbled sentences.

21. Conduct a laughing session.

22. Make ridiculous associations.

23. Let students color with crayons.

24. Draw cartoons to represent concepts.

25. Have students come dressed as one of their parents.

26. Post funny cartoons on the walls in the classroom.

27. Show students some optical illusions.

28. Create riddles about class topics.

29. Have a silly word for the day.

30. Play fun music that relates to the lessons.

31. On Mondays ask for any funny stories from the weekend.

32. Show funny videos from the internet when energy seems low in class.

33. Have a joke of the day.

34. Share Happy Monday Videos, short funny video clips to start the week.

35. Have dress-up days for thematic units.

36. Host a Funny Hat Day.

37. Use relevant comic strips in lessons.

38. Shake like a decaying isotope!

39. Have props to wear during reading.

40. Use puppets.

41. Have an unusual class mascot. Let students name it.

42. When reading aloud, give each character a distinctive voice.

43. Have Terrible Joke Tuesday.

**44.** Have students write a parody.

## EXTENDED IDEAS

**45.** Create a collaborative laugh machine: have everyone force goofy laughter at the same time, and watch as the laughter turns real!

**46.** Play fun review games. Example: have review questions on slips of paper inside inflated balloons. Have students pop the balloons without using their hands or feet. Then read and answer the review questions.

**47.** Have students act out scenes from a story. Make it more challenging by asking them to use no words.

**48.** Ask students to make up a board game about a core concept from class.

**49.** Have a classroom costume/prop box. Bring things out of the box during lessons.

**50.** Have students create a funny commercial based on class topics.

## LANGUAGE OF PLAYFULNESS AND HUMOR

- That's funny!
- Let's play!
- This is fun!
- Have a good time.
- Thanks for a fun day.
- "Laughter"
- Smile!

# DO YOU HAVE ANY MORE IDEAS ON WEAVING "PLAYFULNESS AND HUMOR" INTO YOUR CURRICULUM? IF SO, WRITE THEM HERE!

# BE ORIGINAL

## PRODUCING NOVEL IDEAS AND OUTCOMES.

Have you ever been stuck in a rut? You experience the same routine, day in and day out, as you plug away at the same problem you've been working on for weeks, in the same way you've been working on it since you started. Then, one day, you decide to move away from the obvious and break away from the habits you've been forming. Suddenly, it hits you: the answer to your problem! And it's a completely novel solution.

This skill is about letting go of the obvious and searching for more novel options. And while many teachers may complain that originality has no place in certain classrooms (who wants 2+2 to equal 7?), research has shown that originality is the most widely recognized necessity for creativity,[35] [36] both inside and outside of the classroom.

---

35  Runco, M.A. (1993). Operant theories of insight, originality, and creativity. American Behavioral Scientist, 37(1), 54-67.
36  Runco, M.A. (2004). Creativity. Annual Review of Psychology, 55, 657-687.

When a teacher includes originality in her lessons, whether she is using it as an instruction tool or teaching her students how to *be* more original, she is increasing the likelihood of her students producing more innovative ideas, and being more creative overall.[37] [38] [39] [40]

The following ideas highlight the incorporation of originality into a teaching curriculum and classroom.

## TIPS FOR ENCOURAGING ORIGINALITY IN THE CLASSROOM

1. Have an "It would be great if..." wall in your classroom that students can write on. (i.e. IWBGI we could eat chocolate every day!)

2. Use rubrics that encourage originality.

3. Ask for original responses to your questions.

## QUICK IDEAS

4. Share recipes from different cultures.

---

37  Torrance, E.P. (1972a). Can we teach children to think creatively? Journal of Creative Behavior, 6, 114-143.
38  Torrance, E.P. (1972b). Career patterns and peak creative achievements of creative high school students 12 years later. Gifted Child Quarterly, 16, 75-88.
39  Torrance, E.P. (1972c). Predictive validity of the Torrance Tests of Creative Thinking. Journal of Creative Behavior, 6, 236-252.
40  Torrance, E.P., & Safter, H.T. (1989). The long range predictive validity of the Just Suppose Test. Journal of Creative Behavior, 23, 219-223.

5. Have students write a story or book title.

6. Investigate original questions as a class using the scientific method.

7. Create a Facebook page for a Shakespeare character.

8. Ask students to list ten solutions that don't work. Figure out how to tweak them to make them work.

9. Teach math through stories.

10. Have students find original ways to turn in assignments (no paper or email).

11. Ask students to build their responses to questions out of Lego bricks or Play-Doh.

12. Have students write with their opposite hand.

13. Ask students to write a paragraph backward, like da Vinci did.

14. Give a weekly award for the most original idea.

15. Discuss the originality of fingerprints, butterflies, dogs' faces, etc.

16. Have students come up with a new way to walk.

17. Give each student a piece of paper with the same line on it, then have each of them create a picture out of it.

18. Encourage students to think about a completely new way to travel (by bird, flying shoes, etc.) and reflect on how it might work.

19. Have everyone draw a tree, and discuss how the trees are different.

20. Have students make up their own words for things they don't understand.

21. As a class, take two completely different things and find a way to merge them into one new thing.

22. Have students put two animals or ideas together to create a new animal. Draw the new animal and name it.

23. Ask students to come up with an original way to solve a simple problem (i.e. how to make a peanut butter and jelly sandwich).

24. Re-name the teacher for the day (i.e. Mr. Math).

25. See what problems there are in the classroom (i.e. the window won't open, the wall paint is chipping), and have the students solve them in original ways.

26. Teach about how the names Greenland and Iceland came to be, and rename things to make them more or less appealing.

27. Make paper airplanes and see how different they can all be.

28. Make paper snowflakes and see how different they can all be.

29. Have a tie-dye day.

30. Have students re-name dinosaurs.

31. Encourage students to make up definitions for words they don't know.

32. Teach students about sundials (instead of clocks, phones, or watches) and have them create their own.

33. Discuss: What was the most original thing that you did or that happened to you over the weekend?

34. Ask, What new applications can we find for an already existing product?

35. Give students Lego bricks and have them invent something and present it.

36. Use a random word generator like http://www. randomlists.com/random-words to twist assignments in new directions.

37. Define originality and have students talk about the most original person they know.

38. Have students bring in examples of what is and what is not original. Discuss.

39. Ask, How would nature solve...?

40. Have students think of all the ordinary ways to do a task. Then ask them to do it an unordinary way.

## EXTENDED IDEAS

41. Have students host a talk show interviewing real-life characters.

42. Create a song about fractions.

43. Have students design a new invention.

44. "Build a story" as a class.

45. Break students up into small groups and give each person a small amount of Play-Doh. Give the first

student 30 seconds to make something out of it, explain it, and pass it on. The next student builds onto the object with their Play-Doh for 30 seconds, and so on.

46. Create a class original dance and give it a name. Perform it together.

47. Create an original ending to a story/book read in class.

48. Ask students to build a new writing utensil using Play-Doh.

49. Have students write free verse poetry as a response to famous images from the time period being studied.

50. Take the class on a school safari. Ask students to observe and see things around them as if they have never been there before. Have them ask questions.

"CREATE A CLASS ORIGINAL DANCE AND GIVE IT A NAME. PERFORM IT TOGETHER."

## LANGUAGE OF BEING ORIGINAL

- That is unique!
- Let's look for something new.
- Let's come up with an idea that no one has thought of before.
- Novel
- New
- Unique
- Different

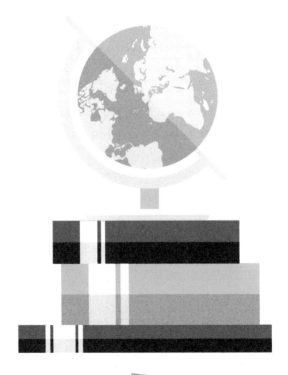

## DO YOU HAVE ANY MORE IDEAS ON WEAVING "BE ORIGINAL" INTO YOUR CURRICULUM? IF SO, WRITE THEM HERE!

# BE AWARE OF EMOTIONS

## UNDERSTANDING WHAT DIFFERENT INDIVIDUALS MAY BE FEELING.

You're talking with a close friend and you notice that things are not quite right. He hasn't said anything, but something about the way that he's sitting and the tone of his voice tells you that something is wrong. You gently ask, "How are you doing?" and the whole story comes pouring out.

This skill is about being conscious of feelings, in yourself and those around you, by recognizing verbal and nonverbal cues and using, trusting, and responding to emotions to better understand people and situations. As a teacher, a large part of your job is to be aware of emotions in order to lead a more open, accepting, and productive classroom. But there is more to this skill than that.

Being aware of emotions is also highly beneficial to the creativity levels of your students.[41] In fact, research shows that emotional factors are more important to creative thinking and breakthrough ideas than logical and intellectual factors.[42] [43] By integrating emotional awareness into your classroom, you will be encouraging a more creative environment.

The following ideas highlight the incorporation of emotional awareness into a teaching curriculum and classroom.

## TIPS FOR ENCOURAGING EMOTIONAL AWARENESS IN THE CLASSROOM

1.  Find ways for students to appropriately express and discuss their emotions.

2.  Encourage an environment where students defer judgment on others' ideas.

3.  Conduct a daily Temperature check. Ten is feeling really good, and one is "I should still be in bed."

41  Sanchez-Ruiz, M.J., Hernandez-Torrano, D., Perez-Gonzalez, J.C., Batey, M., & Petrides, K.V. (2010). The relationship between trait emotional intelligence and creativity across subject domains. Official Journal of the Society for the Study of Motivation, 35(4), 461-473.
42  Torrance, E.P., & Safter, H. T. (1999). Making the Creative Leap Beyond... Buffalo, NY: Creative Education Foundation Press.
43  Gordon, WW (1961). Synectics: The development of creative capacity. New York: Harper & Row.

## QUICK IDEAS

4. On the way out of class, hand each student an exit slip: students rate themselves on a scale of how they feel and how they felt about a lesson.

5. Encourage students to talk about/list feelings before writing responses.

6. Work to make class time less about performance/impressing others and more about sharing your version of the world.

7. Have students debate from choice character perspectives – take different emotional stances.

8. Have a poster in the room with different emotions.

9. Practice gratitude at the end of each school day. Gratitude breeds happiness.

10. Discuss the feelings of various historical people. (How do you think Gandhi felt? What do you think Monet was feeling?)

11. Use examples from movies/books on how characters deal with emotions.

12. Talk about "emotional hijacking" (http://
    lifepsychologyandalotmore.blogspot.com/2008/11/
    emotional-hijacking.html) and how to control it.

13. Ask, what makes you feel better when you're sad?
    Angry? Scared?

14. Read *Alexander and the Terrible, Horrible, No Good,
    Very Bad Day.*

15. Have students list all the things that make them happy.

16. Talk about the positive emotional effects of pets
    and animals.

17. Encourage students to try to remember their dreams
    – what was the strongest emotion present?

18. Show art and ask the students to interpret the
    emotions within the pieces.

19. Have photographs of the different types of emotions
    and have students try to identify what they are.

20. Have students read the same poem in an "unhappy"
    way and then in a "happy" way.

21. Make each student a different emotion. Have them interact with each other at a party (maybe it's "Happy's" birthday party).

22. As a class, make a list of all the ways to express emotion without saying anything.

23. Talk about the psychological environment of the classroom. What makes for a trusting environment?

24. Have a guest come into the class to interact with the teacher. Students need to write down any emotional cues they notice.

25. Pick out several phrases that could be interpreted differently based on the emotional context. Discuss.

26. Ask students to read a passage and become "detectives" and figure out which words indicate how the characters are feeling.

27. Put the students in pairs. Have each student tell the other something about how he or she is feeling in detail. When both students are done, have them share with one another what they heard. Both students may be surprised to hear their feelings summed up in words by someone else.

28. Use this *Symbols of Emotion* exercise: https://app.box. com/s/8tnm1i4o9h248022mbxd

29. Give copies of Plutchik's *Wheel of Emotions* (http:// puix.org/wp-content/uploads/plutchik-wheel-emotion.png) to students, to help them understand their own and others' emotions (including book characters).

30. In teams of two, have students secretly write down an emotion they wish to convey. Then, have each student try to convey that emotion using only facial expressions, then using only gestures, then using words. At the end, have each student reveal the written emotion.

31. Give students color cards that they can wear on their shirts that show their emotional states.

32. Have students look at different advertisements. Which emotions do the advertisements represent?

33. Ask students, "What would you do if you weren't afraid?"

34. Show different movie clips and ask students to decide what emotions are being shown.

35. Have students look at different inanimate and animate objects and try to figure out what emotion it invokes. For example, what does a particular tree outside your window make you feel? Or what does a spoon make you feel?

36. Ask students to imagine the life of a bird. What are all the emotions that a bird feels throughout the course of the day? What are the causes and effects of these emotions?

37. Have a conversation with the class on how emotions affect learning.

## EXTENDED IDEAS

38. Give each student an emotional intelligence cue to observe for the afternoon. Have students make notes at the end of the class regarding their observations, i.e. when people are engaged in the conversation, what are their postures?

39. Give students a skill to practice for the afternoon: smile more, give encouragement to others in the group, listen carefully to someone before commenting, etc. Have these be "secret instructions" at the beginning of class. Afterward ask each student to guess what others were practicing.

40. Have students make playlists of songs for how they handle each emotion.

41. Have a "soundtrack week" – which composer's music sounds the happiest? Saddest? Most tense?

42. Have students pair up and stand face-to-face for 60 seconds in silence while staring into their partners' eyes. Then, have them write out everything that they were thinking and everything they think the other person was thinking. At the end, have the students tear up the papers.

43. Put mood choosers (happy, sad, confused, bored, angry, sick, love-struck, etc.) on each student's notebook, desk, or locker. Students can update their moods and be aware of how they – and others – feel.

44. Stage debates in the class so each participant can see the difference between debate and conflict. Require participants to say "I feel ___" and "I can see that you feel ___" during the dialogue.

45. Narrate an incident without using words. Let your students interpret your story and compare notes.

46. Have students explore emotions using an empathy toy (great for all ages!): http://twentyonetoys.com/pages/empathy-toy

47. Assign a "selfie" project, where each student compiles a chart of emotions using pictures of him or herself.

48. Have students write haikus that describe different emotions.

49. Ask students to chart their emotions as they are going through a challenging project.

50. Have students redesign a lesson in order to maximize their happiness.

ASSIGN A "SELFIE" PROJECT, WHERE EACH STUDENT COMPILES A CHART OF EMOTIONS USING PICTURES OF HIM OR HERSELF.

## LANGUAGE OF EMOTIONAL AWARENESS

- How do you feel about that?
- I am feeling...
- How do you think he/she is feeling?
- I noticed that _____. How are you feeling?

# DO YOU HAVE ANY MORE IDEAS ON WEAVING "BE AWARE OF EMOTIONS" INTO YOUR CURRICULUM? IF SO, WRITE THEM HERE!

# MAKE IT SWING, MAKE IT RING!

## INCORPORATING THE USE OF MOVEMENT AND SOUND.

We all do it: sing in the shower, dance around the living room when nobody's home, tap out a beat on the steering wheel as we drive. We even make up little songs to help us remember a phone number, or to teach our children how to spell their last names. And by doing this, we are enhancing our own creativity, and the creativity of those around us.

This skill is about using our kinesthetic and auditory senses, and responding to sound and movement. Movement and sound are actually fantastic tools to help us warm up our bodies, but they also help us to strengthen and develop our creative minds.[44] [45] This skill is incredibly useful for creative thinking development and, as teachers, we have the opportunity to incorporate it into our classrooms every day.

44  Clarke, A., & Cripps, P. (2012). Fostering creativity: A Multiple Intelligences approach to designing learning in undergraduate fine art. International Journal of Art & Design Education, 31(2), 113-126.
45  Torrance, E.P., & Safter, H. T. (1999). Making the Creative Leap Beyond... Buffalo, NY: Creative Education Foundation Press.

In fact, research has shown that making it swing, or using physical activities and warm-ups, can help students understand, internalize, and remember abstract lessons and information;[46] [47] and making it ring, or using auditory exercises and musical tones, can enhance students' memory and creative expression.[48]

The following ideas highlight the incorporation of making it swing and ring into a teaching curriculum and classroom.

## TIPS FOR USING MAKE IT SWING! MAKE IT RING! IN THE CLASSROOM

1. Be a positive role model for movement in class.

2. Incorporate movement in lessons – moving from desk to desk, going outdoors for a lesson, singing songs with lyrics that match lessons, etc.

3. Encourage students to join choir, band, sports, dance, gymnastics, etc.

---

46  Griss, S. (1994). Creative movement: A language for learning. Educational Leadership, 51, 78-80.
47  White, A.W. (1976). The effects of movement, drawing, and verbal warm-up upon the performance of fourth graders on a figural test of creative thinking. Dissertation Abstracts International, 37, 4248A.
48  Armstrong, T. (1994). Multiple intelligences in the classroom. Alexandria, VA: ASCD.

## QUICK IDEAS

4.  Working in teams of 5-6, have students create any item by using their bodies and making the sound – AKA, acting it out.

5.  Have students stand in a circle with their eyes closed. Tap one person to make a sound. At the end, have everybody open their eyes and guess who made what sound.

6.  Incorporate physical movement related to the essence of a topic or concept.

7.  Have students pose like a sculpture/historical character they're studying.

8.  Let students draw to the rhythm of music.

9.  Use sounds to distinguish urban/suburban/rural/community areas.

10. Show Billy Collins' Ted Talk – Everyday Moments Caught in Time: http://www.ted.com/talks/billy_collins_everyday_moments_caught_in_time

11. Play the mirror game: students pair up, one person leads and one person follows. Students move their bodies and rely on each other to reflect the flow!

12. Create a song based on class concepts or topics.

13. Have students pay attention to the sounds of the lesson.

14. Make the sounds of what it is you are learning about.

15. Ask, What does the Earth sound like?

16. Have students make one physical expression to convey an emotion.

17. Ask students to use their bodies to show knowledge of a topic.

18. Have students move themselves based on debate position.

19. Introduce students to songs that match up with your lesson ("Oliver Cromwell," "We Didn't Start the Fire," the Quadratic Formula song, etc.).

20. Let students play outside on a playground to allow for incubation.

21. Have students play catch while trying to memorize information.

22. Play a "walk this way" game to get the blood flowing, where students have to walk in the same manner as a chosen leader.

23. Do a five-minute movement warm-up before class.

24. Learn brain gym exercises and incorporate them into the classroom.

25. Have students create motions for concepts they can't remember.

26. Allow students to choose how they sit through a lesson.

27. Have students find period music that relates to their favorite historical era.

28. Set up an 8' long 2x4 at the front of the room. Require students to present to the class while standing or walking on the bar.

29. When students have to read something, have them stand up to read.

30. Have students dance like they think a famous person in history would.

31. Ask students to dance a math equation.

32. Have students sing like they think George Washington would have.

33. Teach simple math concepts by clapping numbers and creating rhythms.

34. When learning about places or historical events, have students imagine and then create the sounds and movements that might be associated with the lesson.

## EXTENDED IDEAS

35. Assign a multimedia project where students must use music and recorded sounds and images.

36. Let students use alternative means for handing in assignments – write a rap song, make a video, etc.

37. Prepare a lesson in which students will have to provide sound effects (i.e. rainforest).

38. Create a "soundscape" to depict a concept.

39. Create and play with a live game board.

40. Change the lyrics of a popular song to teach a lesson.

41. Mime out an entire lesson (i.e. photosynthesis).

42. Make up songs to remember key information (address, phone number, spelling out the last name, historical events, etc.).

43. Have a transition song between modules.

44. Have students portray a lesson with only their hands or feet.

45. Ask students to rewrite "We Didn't Start the Fire" to reflect the past 25 years.

46. Do the mp3 experiment with a lesson plan (http://improveverywhere.com/missions/the-mp3-experiments/).

47. Form a conga line for math facts, vocabulary, history dates, or anything they need to memorize.

48. If possible, play music in the background to match the topic (i.e. playing the *Jaws* theme song while studying sharks, or period music when studying history).

49. Have a class hand-shake.

50. Have a 30 second dance party.

## LANGUAGE FOR MAKING IT SWING AND MAKING IT RING

- Did you hear that?
- Listen!
- That sounds like...
- Let's dance!
- Shake it out.
- Let's move.

## DO YOU HAVE ANY MORE IDEAS ON WEAVING "MAKE IT SWING, MAKE IT RING!" INTO YOUR CURRICULUM? IF SO, WRITE THEM HERE!

# KEEP OPEN

## DEFERRING IMMEDIATE JUDGMENT.

**W**hen is the last time that you were collecting ideas for a project that you weren't sure how to approach? Most likely you accepted options with some apathy, until an idea came forward that really stood out to you. "That's it!" you shouted, and ran off to get to work. But was it really the best option, or just the simplest?

This skill is about resisting premature closure and the desire to complete things in the easiest, quickest way. Students especially are prone to premature closure; with the stress of learning new things and struggling to grasp concepts, it's so easy to say, "Yes, that's the one!" However, just because that was the first good solution that came out, that doesn't mean it's the best one – as many creative problem-solving models will confirm.[49]

Keeping open to new ideas is known in the scientific world as one of the most prominent characteristics of a creative

---

49  Torrance, E.P., & Safter, H. T. (1999). Making the Creative Leap Beyond... Buffalo, NY: Creative Education Foundation Press.

person.[50] [51] As teachers, we can encourage openness by reminding students to defer their judgment – both positive and negative – and wait until all of the options are on the table before trying to choose one. Openness is also highly praised in creative relationships, such as that between the teacher and student. When openness is present, the two individuals are allowing for a higher level of relating to one another,[52] which is highly important for the safe environment that every teacher strives to provide in his classroom.

The following ideas highlight the incorporation of keeping open into a teaching curriculum and classroom.

## TIPS FOR ENCOURAGING OPENNESS IN THE CLASSROOM

1.  Find joy in the process.

2.  Keep asking, "What else?"

3.  Teach the concept of deferring judgment.

4.  Relax, listen, and understand.

50  Davis (1992). Creativity is forever (3rd ed.). Dubuque, IA: Kendall-Hunt.
51  Rogers, C.R. (1979). Freedom to learn. London: Charles C. Merrill.
52  Moustakas, C.E. (1977). Creative life. New York, NY: Wiley & Sons, Inc.

## QUICK IDEAS

5. Hang a "Keep Open" sign on your door.

6. Present a bad idea, and ask students to keep open and find one thing they like about it first.

7. Encourage students to brainstorm new possibilities by deferring judgment.

8. Take on complex problems and focus on where to start.

9. Introduce math problems that can be solved in more than one way.

10. Wear an unusual item of clothing and ask students what they like about it.

11. Have students put a pen to paper and create a picture without lifting the pen.

12. Try an experiment that has the potential to work (or not). Ask the students to keep open.

13. Play *Pass the Poem* – each student writes a line based only on the line previous to his or her own (the rest are covered up or folded over). The teacher writes the first line.

14. Literally keep things open (i.e. windows, doors, books) to see what other things come in (i.e. leaves, wind, people, dust). Use this as a metaphor for open minds and ideas.

15. Have students do an exercise where they have to end every sentence with "and..."

16. Talk about something that will never be finished or completed.

17. Make students list 20 ideas for a project or activity before choosing one.

18. When asking questions, don't take the first answer as being correct – ask students to think of alternative answers. Teach them that there isn't always only one way to look at things.

19. Find stories or fables to share about people who stopped too soon or took the easiest route to help encourage exploration.

20. Have a mistake quotient each day – the number of times they should try and keep trying.

21. Blindfold the students. Give them each an object that has an unusual texture, smell, shape, etc. Have them imagine all the possibilities of what it might be.

22. Use improvisation to encourage openness to new situations.

23. Play *Pass the Draw* – teams of two pass a drawing back and forth, adding to it each time and changing the picture however they see fit.

24. Start with a very zoomed-in photo and incrementally zoom out. At each stage, have students propose what the photo might be.

25. Experiment with ideas as a class without expecting an outcome.

26. Have posters in the room of ideas that were once rejected but are now widely accepted.

27. Have case studies related to the lessons that are based on stories of people whose ideas at first didn't work but now do (i.e. Angry Birds).

28. Get students to imagine impossibilities (i.e. people being able to fly, quadruped animals walking on two feet, etc.).

29. Play a short video clip up until the moment of conflict. Have students discuss possible resolutions or outcomes.

30. Explore Wikipedia as a class to find a good starting point and then follow random links. Make connections between random page and your problem or topic. As a debriefing, encourage students to look for ideas in unlikely places.

31. Have a mismatch clothing day in class.

32. Encourage students to experiment with two very different (safe) materials and see what they can make.

33. Play foreign music that students may not have heard before. Ask students to keep open about it.

34. Have one student tell a story in gibberish. Ask the other students to guess what the story is about, based on tone of voice and body language.

35. Explore different ways of solving a math problem.

36. Conduct a breathing exercise. Have students scrunch into a ball and take a deep breath. Then have them take a breath when they are standing up straight

with good posture. Use this to explain openness to new ideas.

37. Play *Simon Says*, but swap the rules. Instead of performing the actions that "Simon" instructs, students must only perform the actions that are not preceded by "Simon Says."

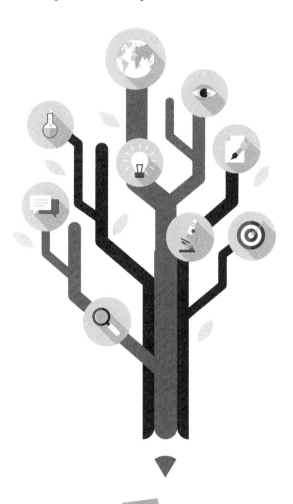

## EXTENDED IDEAS

38. Find a book with an unattractive cover and a great story. Ask students for their reactions to the book before and after reading it.

39. Have students debate a perspective that opposes their own.

40. Encourage students to practice listening to one another without thinking about how they want to respond.

41. Have a blindfolded taste-testing (allergies permitting) of new foods. After you tell them what it is, ask the students if they would have tried it on their own.

42. Teach two opposing scientific theories. Have a debate where students *must* point out what makes sense about the other argument before responding.

43. Give students a project. Each day, do a progress check and then change the rules (or change the game) a little bit to make them reconsider. Remind them that it's normal to be frustrated by not having it done, but that's a part of the world we live in.

44. Give each student one item to add to their sculpture project each day. Have them visualize the final

product in advance (tell the class what they are making) but not finish it right away.

45. Have a defer judgment jar. When a student hears an idea that he does not like, he writes down the idea and his concerns and puts it in the jar. *After* discussing the positives, the jar can be opened.

46. Have students come to class with the worst ideas imaginable related to the topic at hand, and then get people to find what's good about them.

47. Work with a colleague in a different subject area and teach a lesson together (i.e. the Cold War from a scientific perspective).

48. Give students materials to make a picture, and ask them to create continuously without planning the final outcome.

49. Go outside and play soccer, basketball, etc. Show students that when they stay open on the field, they are more likely to get the ball. Make the connection to thinking.

50. Have students write stories up until the climax. Then, ask them to swap stories and finish each others' works.

## LANGUAGE FOR KEEPING OPEN

- Defer judgment.
- Stay open to possibilities.
- Let's not make a decision yet!
- Let's give it some time.

## DO YOU HAVE ANY MORE IDEAS ON WEAVING "KEEP OPEN" INTO YOUR CURRICULUM? IF SO, WRITE THEM HERE!

....................................................................

....................................................................

....................................................................

....................................................................

....................................................................

....................................................................

....................................................................

....................................................................

....................................................................

....................................................................

....................................................................

# GET **GLIMPSES** OF THE FUTURE

## IMAGINING WHAT HAS YET TO COME.

**W**here do you see yourself in ten years? How about twenty? Now, where do you see your students in ten and twenty years? What new technologies do you think will be coming out? Will your students be inventors, politicians, activists, writers? Will they go to college or get jobs right out of school? Will the future be bright for them – and will they make the future bright?

This skill is about predicting, imagining, and exploring opportunities and situations that do not yet exist. Research shows that envisioning the future makes students more likely to pursue, and even master, the problems they wish to solve and the goals they wish to achieve.[53] [54] [55] In

53   de Brabandere, L., & Iny, A. (2010). Scenarios and creativity: Thinking in new boxes. Technological Forecasting and Social Change, 77(9), 1506-1512.
54   Isham, D. (1997). Developing a computerized interactive visualization assessment. Journal of Computer-Aided Environmental Design and Education, 3(1), 1-15.
55   Torrance, E.P., & Safter, H. T. (1999). Making the Creative Leap Beyond... Buffalo, NY: Creative Education Foundation Press.

short, visualization encourages both artistic and scientific creativity in students and vice versa.[56] [57]

As teachers, it is especially essential for us to highlight the importance of this skill for our students. By envisioning and glimpsing a future that might be, students may be more encouraged to turn that vision into a reality. If we never show them that the future is theirs, they may not know what to do with it once they get there.

The following ideas highlight the incorporation of getting glimpses of the future into a teaching curriculum and classroom.

## TIPS FOR GETTING GLIMPSES OF THE FUTURE IN THE CLASSROOM

1. Bring in telescopes, binoculars, and kaleidoscopes to get into the explorative and creative mindset.

---

56  Allen, A.D. (2010). Complex spatial skills: The link between visualization and creativity. Creativity Research Journal, 22(3), 241-249.
57  Kozhevnikov, M., Kozhevnikov, M., Yu, C.J., & Blazhenkova, O. (2013). Creativity, visualization abilities, and visual cognitive style. British Journal of Educational Psychology, 83, 196-209.

## QUICK IDEAS

2. Ask, What is a futurist? Have students name several futurists.

3. Play the "What if?" game as a class. For example, what if teleportation existed? What effects would that have?

4. Ask, What will not change in the future? Why not?

5. As a class, read a few articles from *Save Tomorrow for the Children*.[58] Student predictions in this book are describing 2010, written in 1980. Were the students on target about today's world? How do you envision tomorrow's world, 20 years from now?

6. Ask, "What did your neighborhood look like _____ years ago? What does it look like now? What will it look like in _____ years?" Have students draw pictures or use a computer.

7. Bring in a crystal ball, and have students talk about what they see happening in five years.

8. Give everyone a time wand. When they wave it around, presto! It's ten years from now. What's happening?

---

58   Torrance, E.P., Weiner, D., & Presbury, J.H. (1987). Save tomorrow for the children. Buffalo, NY: Bearly Ltd.

9.  Ask the students what a building would look like in the future if it behaved like a tree (captured carbon, released oxygen, added to the beauty of the neighborhood, etc.).

10. Have students make a list of things that don't exist yet.

11. Encourage students to imagine a student trying to solve the same problem in 50 years. How would he solve it? What tools would she use?

12. Let students 'be' a weather pattern. How might they change things?

13. Have students wish up new apps and computer programs.

14. Listen to students' ideas about the community. What are some things that might fix a problem, bring new jobs, or provide something new in the future?

15. Similar to Sleeping Beauty or Rip Van Winkle, have students imagine that they have been asleep for 100, 500, or 1000 years. Ask them to draw a picture of what the world might look like when they wake up.

16. Read *Choose Your Own Adventure* stories in class.

17. Have students find science-fiction stories to relate to the topic you're talking about and get them to think about what the implications are.

18. Ask students to write letters to themselves in a year outlining the goals they would like to achieve in the course, and then mail them the letters a year later.

19. Have current magazines in your classroom so students can peruse them and then discuss the effect that what is happening now will have in the future.

20. Get students in groups to read about any emerging technology or social trends, then apply them to work out the implications in a different context.

21. As a class, look for people who are already living in the future (future of fashion, trends, etc.)

22. Read futurist blog posts and bring them into the class.

23. Have students look for trending topics on Twitter and try to predict what will happen next week.

24. Ask students to imagine how people will listen to music in the future (history shows records, 8track, cassettes, CDs, iPods, and The Cloud).

25. Teach mathematics in the context of huge data sets. Think about solving mathematical problems when Google knows everything. What is the role of a human mathematician?

26. Have students think about how we might be communicating with one another in five years? Ten years? Will we even have words, or will there be other means to communicate?

27. Think about what the classroom will be like in ten years. What will be the best ways students will learn? Set up the classroom to reflect your class's vision.

28. Have students imagine the first person landing on Mars. What does the planet look like from his/her perspective?

29. Ask, How would you communicate with the first alien life form that Earth encounters? What do you think would be the most important things to share with the alien about our world?

30. Ask, "What would you do with your life if you knew you would live to be 1000? What would be the effect on society?"

31. Have students think about all of the robots they might want to make life easier.

32. Ask, "What would be the ideal sport to play in space?"

## EXTENDED IDEAS

33. As a class, take a look at books like *The Extreme Future* by James Canton. Think about what the future might be like.

34. Write or draw what might come after the Age of Technology. Have students name the next one or two ages that will come over the next thousand years.

35. Have "Future Week" and each day hold a project like: Design a future car or transportation machine, Design a future pair of shoes, Design a future hairstyle and fashionable clothes, Describe the sound of future music, Describe life on a space outpost or colonized planet, etc.

36. Have students write a magazine article dated ten years from now.

37. Ask students to pretend they are from a past age, and ask them to look at today's ordinary things – phones, cars, video games, etc. Have them dress up in a costume of the past and touch, pick up, and use those things.

38. Use cartoon storyboarding as a tool to help students imagine five steps ahead – if it looks like this today (cell 1) what will it look like ten years from now (cell 6)?

39. Encourage students to go to places that allow them to wonder – like the planetarium, the forest, an art museum, etc.

40. Ask students to plan a (realistic or not) class field trip.

41. At the beginning of the school year, have each student write a prediction of his or her learning/engagement outcomes and seal it in an envelope. At the end of the year, return the envelopes to the students and discuss the results.

42. Have a class reunion where everyone comes into the classroom as themselves in five or 10 years.

43. Encourage students to invent futures by using video games like The Sims.

44. Have students invent a product or service that will need to exist ten years in the future. Allow them to imagine the parts that aren't currently possible.

45. Ask students to invent musical instruments that might exist in the future.

46. As a class, add 20 new words to the dictionary for objects and situations that don't yet exist.

47. Have students write a prophecy for the future.

48. As a class, invent retronyms for things that will need to be explained to a future generation (for example, a rotary phone was a phone until there were mobile phones).

49. Ask students to build a model of a form of transportation for the year 2115.

50. Have students create commercials for future products.

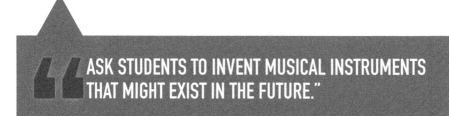

ASK STUDENTS TO INVENT MUSICAL INSTRUMENTS THAT MIGHT EXIST IN THE FUTURE."

## LANGUAGE FOR GETTING GLIMPSES OF THE FUTURE

- Let's think about the future.
- Imagine what _____ might be like.
- Predict...
- Envision...
- What do you foresee?

# DO YOU HAVE ANY MORE IDEAS ON WEAVING "GET GLIMPSES OF THE FUTURE" INTO YOUR CURRICULUM? IF SO, WRITE THEM HERE!

........................................................................................

........................................................................................

........................................................................................

........................................................................................

........................................................................................

........................................................................................

........................................................................................

........................................................................................

........................................................................................

........................................................................................

........................................................................................

# BREAK THROUGH AND EXTEND THE BOUNDARIES

## THINKING OUTSIDE THE PRESCRIBED REQUIREMENTS.

Have you ever had a student who was perfectly content to give run-of-the-mill answers to intriguing questions? Sure, the answers were applicable and solved the problems at hand, but they lacked the innovation and excitement that you were after. Then one day, in frustration, you told the student to "think outside the box" – and he astounded you with an answer that was completely out of left field!

This skill is about thinking outside of the prescribed requirements. You may know it better by the statement, "think outside the box" – but we want you to think of it as more than just a go-to phrase. Expanding the boundaries is a skill that everyone possesses; it is about shattering the limits that have been defined for us. This skill can be developed and honed through practice, and is integral to creativity and problem solving.[59] [60]

As teachers, it may be difficult for us to include this type of thinking in our lessons and classrooms. Many of us have guidelines to follow and tests to which we must teach. However, thinking outside of the prescribed requirements, and taking the focus away from analytical skills alone, can open our students up to innovative thinking and solutions to common problems, solutions that even we had not considered.[61] [62] [63]

The following ideas highlight the incorporation of keeping open into a teaching curriculum and classroom.

## TIPS FOR BREAKING THROUGH AND EXTENDING THE BOUNDARIES IN THE CLASSROOM

1. Ask "What if ____?" at least three times every day.

2. Ask students to pretend there are no limits to what they can do before coming up with solutions or ideas.

59  Blendinger, J., & McGrath, V. (2000). Thinking outside the box: A self-teaching guide for educational leaders. ED441874.
60  Gibbons, J. & Gray, M. (2004). Critical thinking as integral to social work practice. Journal of Teaching in Social Work, 24(1-2), 19-38.
61  Deacon, S. & Thomas, V. (2000). Discovering creativity in family therapy: A theoretical analysis. Journal of Systematic Therapies, 19(3), 4-17.
62  Ringel, S. (2003). The reflective self: A path to creativity and intuitive knowledge in social work practice education. Journal of Teaching in Social Work, 23(3/4), 15–28.
63  Starko, A. (1995). Creativity in the classroom. New York: Longman Publications.

3. When students have a problem, ask the questions, "Why?" and "What's stopping you?"

## QUICK IDEAS

4. Provide five unrelated items and have students find connections between them.

5. Ask students to "take away" one of the five senses – how are the others enhanced?

6. Draw a circle on the floor and have everyone stand inside it. To get out, each student has to come up with a new use for a broom.

7. Tell students to imagine that they are all in a box. Have them come up with novel ways to get out of the box.

8. If you want to think outside the box, first make a list of everything that is IN THE BOX.

9. As a class, practice connecting things that don't belong together.

10. Take flash cards that associate "like" things and cut them up.

11. Make the last question of a test, "Is there anything on this test that you would like to question?"

12. Put the chairs in the classroom in any way but rows.

13. Have a student sit in the teacher's desk one day a week.

14. Play MadLibs as a class.

15. Use a rubber band to show that boundaries can be expanded further than we might originally think.

16. Introduce the Nine Dots puzzle: http://www.permadi.com/fpcgi/9dots/

17. Encourage students to think about what would happen if there were one less constraint when solving a problem.

18. Have students pick a superhero and think about how he/she might solve the problem.

19. Give students a complex math problem but not a way to solve it.

20. Ask students to think about a historical event. Imagine what else might have been happening that wasn't captured in words.

21. Invite students to sit for a lesson in a way that they feel comfortable (i.e. on the floor, sitting on desks, etc.).

22. Surprise your students by having class in an unusual room in the building (i.e. science in the gym).

23. Teach a math class in the swimming pool.

24. As a class, make a list of words that have different meanings in different cultures.

25. Move the chairs and tables around the classroom in an unusual way. Debrief on what it felt like to sit outside the normal paradigm.

## EXTENDED IDEAS

26. Highlight biomimicry: use ideas from nature to design solutions.

27. Give an ambiguous problem (i.e. What is the sound of one hand clapping?) with no instructions to solve the problem. Ask students to present their answers to the class after a week, in two minutes or less.

28. Ask students to write a poem – without using pen, pencil, chalk, markers, computer, paper, or any traditional writing materials at all.

29. Have students figure out how something is made and report on it.

30. Ask students to consider a familiar sport and create a whole new set of rules for the game that will radically change how the game is played and scored. Envision new equipment if need be.

31. Have class outside under a tree. Reflect on the experience of expanding the physical learning space.

32. Combine different grades/age groups and teach a lesson that they all will understand and enjoy. Have them discuss what they learned from each perspective.

33. Have each student create a story to share around a certain topic. While creating the story, have each student reach into a bag of unusual objects and weave the chosen object into the story.

34. Stretch a large sheet of plastic wrap between two posts and ask students to get through it. After they all struggle to do so, discuss the focus and creativity that is necessary in order to truly break through the boundaries.

35. Give students a drawing and ask them to color in the negative space to bring the drawing to life.

36. Ask students to think about the worst possible way to solve a problem, and then make it even worse. Encourage them to think about what it says about the problem and what ideas it gives them.

37. Use the SCAMPER technique (Substitute, Combine, Adapt, Modify, Put to another Use, Eliminate, Reverse).[64]

38. Have students imagine a problem that had to be solved within the next hour, otherwise the world would end. How would they solve it?

39. Encourage students to create new music by mashing up recordings of at least three different styles of music.

40. Give a test that doesn't have any "right" answers. Let creativity count!

41. Give a test that has all the answers but grade students on how interesting their questions can be.

42. Ask students to write essays based entirely on stream of consciousness. What did they notice that they did not see before?

43. Get students to pick a word at random from the dictionary and to create some sort of art that reflects it.

64 Eberle, B. (2008). SCAMPER: Creative games and activities for imagination development. Waco, TX: Prufrock Press.

44. Give students a cardboard box and ask them to think of all the ways it is not a box. Introduce the children's book, *Not a Box.*[65]

45. Ask all the students to write down the worst idea they can think of. Hand them around at random and ask everyone to come up with at least three things they like about the ideas.

46. Have students invent a new alphabet and try to communicate with it.

47. Ask students to look for solutions to problems in books that have no relevance.

48. Get students to play the roles of cells and enzymes in the body.

49. Have a Bring-your-grandparent-to-school Day, where the students and grandparents work on problems together.

50. Ban writing for a day. Students can only communicate visually.

---

65  Portis, A. (2011). Not a box. New York, NY: Harper Collins.

## LANGUAGE FOR BREAKING THROUGH AND EXTENDING THE BOUNDARIES

- Go beyond...
- Color outside the lines.
- Think past the obvious.
- What else?

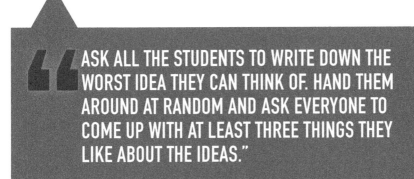

ASK ALL THE STUDENTS TO WRITE DOWN THE WORST IDEA THEY CAN THINK OF. HAND THEM AROUND AT RANDOM AND ASK EVERYONE TO COME UP WITH AT LEAST THREE THINGS THEY LIKE ABOUT THE IDEAS."

## DO YOU HAVE ANY MORE IDEAS ON WEAVING "BREAK THROUGH AND EXTEND THE BOUNDARIES" INTO YOUR CURRICULUM? IF SO, WRITE THEM HERE!

# TOLERATE THE AMBIGUITY

## EMBRACING THE UNKNOWN.

Think about the last time you were told, "It's a surprise!" How did you handle that? Did you start snooping around, trying to get more information from wherever you could find it? Did you beg and plead for a giveaway from someone you knew was involved? Or did you accept the unknown and let things unfold the way they were meant to?

This skill is about being able to embrace uncertainties. Most of us get uncomfortable when we don't know what's going to happen – the possibilities become endless, and that can become overwhelming. However, teaching your students to embrace uncertainties can actually heighten their levels of creativity.[66] [67] [68] In fact, research shows that the tolerance

66  Barron, F., & Harrington, D. M. (1981). Creativity, intelligence, and personality. Annual Review of Psychology, 32, 439-476.
67  Golann, S. E. (1963). Psychological study of creativity. Psychological Bulletin, 60, 548-565.
68  Sternberg, R. J., & Lubart, T. I. (1995). Defying the crowd: Cultivating creativity in a culture of conformity. New York, NY: Free Press.

of ambiguity encourages effective work on a larger set of problems, as well as the optimization of creative potential.[69]

As teachers, it is our goal to empower students to accomplish as much as they can. By incorporating this skill into lesson plans and classroom environments, we can heighten our students' creative self-efficacies,[70] as well as their desires to explore the new, unusual, and complex.[71]

The following ideas highlight the incorporation of tolerating the ambiguity into a teaching curriculum and classroom.

## TIPS FOR TOLERATING THE AMBIGUITY IN THE CLASSROOM

1. Remind students that you don't know all the answers.

2. Reward students for showing how they tackled ambiguous problems.

---

69  Vernon, P. E. (1970): Creativity: Selected readings. Harmondsworth, Middlesex, England: Penguin.
70  Wang, S., Zhang, X., & Martocchio, J. (2011). Thinking outside of the box when the box is missing: Role ambiguity and its linkage to creativity. Creativity Research Journal, 23(3), 211-221.
71  Urban, K. K. (2003). Toward a Componential Model of Creativity. In D. Ambrose, L. M. Cohen, & A.J. Tannenbaum (Eds.) Creative Intelligence: Toward Theoretic Integration. Cresskill, NJ: Hampton Press Inc.

## QUICK IDEAS

3.  Ask students to tolerate the ambiguity for the lesson, and give them very vague instructions. Debrief with them on how it felt, what they did to tolerate ambiguity, and what they can do better next time.

4.  Give students minimal information and have them work through the complexity of the content.

5.  Put a chair in the middle of the doorway. Will the students move it, wait in the hall, or walk around?

6.  Take away the chairs in a classroom.

7.  Hold a classroom election or contest. Wait a week to reveal the results.

8.  As soon as class starts, tell the students they're on their own to learn the lesson. Have some notes on the board, but not many. Do not provide instruction or leadership – and see what happens!

9.  Show the clip from *Apollo 13* where the NASA workers have to solve a problem on the spaceship from Mission Control, using only the supplies that the astronauts have in the ship.

10. Have students work on an assignment, and then halfway through have them switch groups and finish the other group's project.

11. Take something apart and bring it to class. Ask students to try to guess what all the pieces made before they were taken apart.

12. Make a class list of things you don't know.

13. Assign groups or partners randomly for activities and projects.

14. End classes with cliff-hangers so students leave wondering what the answer is and have to wait until they return the next day to find out.

15. Watch the "Big Bang Theory" clip where Amy helps Sheldon cope with compulsive closure: https://www.youtube.com/watch?v=Z3z_yZ1G1Og

16. Incorporate Mystery Tubes into your lesson plan: http://undsci.berkeley.edu/lessons/mystery_tubes.html

17. Ask your students, "What's the worst-case scenario? Can you live with that?"

18. Get students to identify their levels of certainty around various facts.

19. Ask students to imagine what the problem would look like if they let go of their certainty around facts.

20. Encourage students to guess when they don't know the answer and to explore the implications if these guessed answers were facts.

21. Tell students there will be a big surprise during the following class, but don't tell them what it will be.

22. Encourage students to invent ideas without worrying about whether or not they will be able to make them work.

23. Have students come up with the most ambiguous question they can and then think about how they might start to answer it.

24. Give a case study or example of how scientists often start with ambiguous problems.

25. Give students a big jigsaw puzzle without the picture.

26. Have students play PowerPoint karaoke. You control the slides as they present the material, and they don't know what's coming next.

27. Give your students the instructions for an activity, but leave some of the words blank.

28. Give students a big bag of Lego bricks (or a pile of newspapers or recyclable materials) and tell them to construct something related to the lesson.

29. During a break, play a game with a ball as a class, but make up the rules as you go.

30. Give students a folder with the contents of the lesson/course, with the label "Do Not Open" across the top.

31. Place a lesson-related object under students' chairs, but don't let them look until the end of the lesson.

32. Start telling a story and schedule an interrupting phone call in the middle. After the phone call, don't finish the story. Resume teaching.

33. Place objects around the room and ask students not to touch them. Do not give any other information.

## EXTENDED IDEAS

34. Give a small project with instructions that the project will be graded, but students are not allowed to know

what the project will be graded on. Present this as fun so they won't panic about it. Grade for something simple like "done on time," "depth of thought," "use of color," or "presented with a smile" so everyone gets a good grade.

35. Have teams of two or three students do rock-balancing sculptures outside and predict which ones will make it through a rainy night.

36. Incorporate gardening or planting in the classroom. Will the plants blossom? Will we have a harvest?

37. Ambiguous characters: Show the class a frozen YouTube video with a person in the frame. Have them speculate on what is about to happen, what voice or accent the character will have, and anything else they can add to the scenario. At the end, play the video to see if they were close. Repeat this several times with very short descriptions.

38. Play 20 Questions with pertinent information from your lesson plan.

39. Play Wheel of Fortune with names of people or places from lessons.

40. Tape the name of a historical figure on each student's

back, and have them ask questions about their characters until they guess who they are.

41. Have students say what they are most uncertain about. Talk about what would happen if they never became certain about it.

42. Give ambiguous answers to all questions. When students notice, debrief.

43. Play a game similar to the TV series "Chopped" where there are mystery ingredients in the basket that students will have to use to solve a problem or design a product. There is always one ingredient that is difficult to use.

44. Change things around in the classroom every month – shift the desks, put them in different configurations, change the room to face another direction, add different elements, etc.

45. Take students through a story or scene where you take parts away and see how it changes. Each time, ask the students how it made them feel.

46. Have students construct an assignment that involves a lifelong endeavor, the future of which is unknown.

47. Teach an entire class without speaking – only use slides, whiteboard, chalkboard, etc. During your next class, teach tolerance of ambiguity.

48. Leave an empty space in your syllabus called Tolerate the Ambiguity so that students won't know everything that's going to happen.

49. When working on a challenging assignment, tell students to stop what they're doing in the middle of the assignment to take a few deep breaths and think about what they want to do next.

50. Give students wrapped presents. Tell them they can't open them until the end of the week.

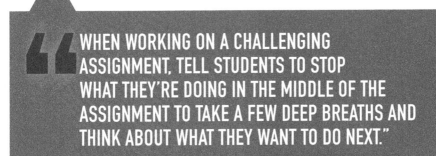

**WHEN WORKING ON A CHALLENGING ASSIGNMENT, TELL STUDENTS TO STOP WHAT THEY'RE DOING IN THE MIDDLE OF THE ASSIGNMENT TO TAKE A FEW DEEP BREATHS AND THINK ABOUT WHAT THEY WANT TO DO NEXT."**

## LANGUAGE FOR TOLERATING THE AMBIGUITY

- Let's wait and see.
- Let's work through it.
- What don't we know?
- Stay open to possibilities.
- How might this turn out?

## DO YOU HAVE ANY MORE IDEAS ON WEAVING "TOLERATE THE AMBIGUITY" INTO YOUR CURRICULUM? IF SO, WRITE THEM HERE!

......................................................................

......................................................................

......................................................................

......................................................................

......................................................................

......................................................................

......................................................................

......................................................................

......................................................................

......................................................................

......................................................................

# PUT IDEAS INTO CONTEXT

## APPLYING WHAT YOU HAVE LEARNED.

Think back to when you yourself were a student. Was there ever a concept in school that you simply could not grasp? The teacher would try to explain it in different ways, but it just never clicked – that is, until your teacher decided to put the concept into a context that was meaningful to you.

This skill is about putting smaller parts or experiences into a larger framework or putting things together in meaningful ways. It's all well and good to encourage creative thinking in your students – but they, like all people, have an innate desire to understand the world around them[72] and, by adding relatable context to your lessons, you will be encouraging their creativity and strengthening their intrinsic motivation. [72] [73] [74]

---

72  Torrance, E.P., & Safter, H. T. (1999). Making the Creative Leap Beyond... Buffalo, NY: Creative Education Foundation Press.
73  Hoyt, K.B. (1975). Career education in transition: Trends and implications for the future. Columbus, OH: ERIC Clearing House on Adult, Career, and Vocational Education: National Center for Research in Vocational Education, Ohio State University.
74  Hoyt, (1989). The career status of women and minority persons: A 20-year retrospective. The Career Development Quarterly, 37(3), 202-212.

As teachers, we are responsible for helping to shape and nurture the minds of the future. And in order for these minds to have genuinely creative ideas and further advance the human race, they must possess the human ability to put ideas into context.[75]

We have not listed any ideas for you to practice putting ideas into context. Instead, we want to ask you:

*How might you incorporate the skills and concepts in this book into your classroom and your everyday life? Write your ideas on the next page!*

**Want to further extend your ability to put creativity into context by taking a deep dive into (re)designing your curriculum to include creativity skills? Take a look at our Facebook page for more information on our colleague Susan Keller-Mathers' work on weaving creativity into content with the Torrance Incubation Model, coming out in Fall 2015.**

---

75  Fuller (1974). Intuition. In P.W. Garlan, M. Dunstari, & D.H. Pike (Eds.) Star sigh: Visions of the future. Englewood Cliffs, NJ: Prentice-Hall.

**NOTES:**

....................................................................................

....................................................................................

....................................................................................

....................................................................................

....................................................................................

....................................................................................

....................................................................................

....................................................................................

....................................................................................

....................................................................................

....................................................................................

....................................................................................

# ABOUT THE AUTHORS

Dr. Cyndi Burnett is an Assistant Professor at the International Center for Studies in Creativity at Buffalo State. She has a Bachelor of Fine Arts in Theater, a Master of Science in Creativity, and a Doctorate of Education in Curriculum, Teaching and Learning, all of which she uses to help "ignite creativity around the world." Her research interests include: the use of creative models and techniques with children, creative thinking in higher education, and current trends in creativity. Her work includes projects such as: working with educators to bring creative thinking into the classroom, connecting communities of creative thinkers via social media, and designing and running a Massive Open Online Course (MOOC) on Everyday Creativity.

Dr. Burnett was featured in an article in the New York Times titled, "Creativity Becomes an Academic Discipline." She is the co-editor of the *Big Questions* in Creativity book series and co-author of the book *My Sandwich is a Spaceship: Creative Thinking for Parents and Young Children*.

Website: www.CyndiBurnett.com
Faculty Page: http://creativity.buffalostate.edu/faculty/cynthia-burnett
Massive Open Online Course in Creativity: https://class.coursera.org/creative-001
Online Course on Creative Thinking in the Classroom: http://udemy.com/the-creative-thinking-course-for-teachers
Twitter: @CyndiBurnett
Facebook: https://www.facebook.com/cyndiaburnett
Email: Cyndi.burnett@gmail.com

Julia Figliotti is a Creative Specialist at Knowinnovation, an international facilitation company with a focus on scientific innovation. With a Bachelor of Arts in Writing and a Master of Science in Creativity, she specializes in academic writing and story telling. She has been published with National Public Radio, The Partnership for 21st Century Skills, *Big Questions in Creativity 2014*, and *Gargoyle* magazine. Julia's projects include the co-design and management of a Massive Open Online Course (MOOC) on Everyday Creativity and the technical assistance for numerous innovation workshops.

Website: http://knowinnovation.com/our-team/julia-figliotti/
LinkedIn: https://www.linkedin.com/in/juliafigliotti
Email: julia.figliotti@knowinnovation.com

CPSIA information can be obtained at www.ICGtesting.com
Printed in the USA
BVOW05s1027040816

457882BV00031B/184/P